Home Office

Drug Misusers and the Criminal Justice System

Part II:
Police, Drug Misusers
and the
Community

Report by the Advisory Council on the Misuse of Drugs

London: HMSO

Contents

Chapter

Appendices

The Advisory Council on the Misuse of Drugs

Members

1. Introduction and Overview

1.1 Tackling drug misuse involves both reducing the supply of and demand for drugs. We have no doubt about the importance of the enforcement role, particularly that of the police, in dealing with drug misuse. It is a vital element of the overall strategy along with prevention, treatment and rehabilitation. At the same time, we are convinced that policing objectives and public expectations must be realistic. Elimination of drug misuse is generally regarded as an unobtainable goal. The immediate objective must be to influence and contain the scale and nature of misuse. Even containment will involve considerable effort and resources but we are satisfied that much can be done.

The Criminal Justice Working Group

1.2 A brief summary of the background of the Criminal Justice Working Group is given in Appendix A. The Working Group's membership has a broad range of relevant experience and expertise (Appendix B). In addition to senior police officers, the Working Group includes academics, representatives from the medical profession, probation service, the courts, as well as members with considerable experience of drug services and the treatment of misusers. In producing this report we received a considerable volume of evidence from police forces and other organisations, both statutory and voluntary, and from academics (Appendix C).

Scope of the Report

1.3 In this second stage of our work we have been looking at enforcement and prosecution issues relating to the local policing of drug misuse. Drugs enforcement involves other agencies besides the police, most notably HM Customs and Excise. Our focus here is not with the response to high-level drug crime, such as large scale dealing and trafficking. Our interest is with the interactions between misusers and enforcement and prosecution agencies, drugs services and the community at large, and with the extent to which there is scope for reducing the supply and demand for drugs and the harm they cause to individuals and society. We have endeavoured to recognise the limitations on our enquiries. For example, we have not considered the complex management and resource issues that the police face in responding to drug misuse since these fall within the executive authority of the police.

Overview

1.4 We were struck by the complexity of much of police involvement in dealing with drug misuse, and related crime, perhaps more so than in the enforcement of most other areas of the criminal law. In addition to carrying out their traditional role of reducing the supply of drugs, the police are becoming increasingly involved in reducing demand and in doing so are tailoring their strategies to accommodate wider objectives including those concerned with individual welfare and public health. This wider involvement often presents police forces with competing and even conflicting priorities.

1.5 These varied demands have led a growing number of police forces to adopt harm reduction principles in developing their policing strategies. Since the advent of AIDS, harm reduction has become a well respected and well understood approach to tackling drug misuse. Harm reduction principles are not incompatible with vigorous street policing, indeed in many circumstances they actually require it. We commend the development of policing strategies which aim to limit the harms caused by drug misuse. This implies a recognition that the enforcement of laws against drug misuse cannot wholly eliminate misuse but a variety of policing approaches can have a limiting effect on the level of harm caused to individuals and to society. This strategy is sometimes called community damage limitation and we use both terms in the Report to ensure the widest understanding of these developments.

1.6 The harm reduction approach requires the establishment of effective links between the police and the community as well as good inter-agency co-operation. We recognise the considerable difficulties that may prevent this co-operation being more than simply cosmetic. The underlying issue is the difficulty of the police and other agencies establishing a common purpose, given the different philosophies with which traditionally the police and drug agencies have approached drug misuse. Adoption of a shared agenda would recognise the common purpose of all the agencies involved as being to minimise the harm caused by drug misuse to the individual in so far as this is compatible with community safety and the public interest. Progress requires a shift in approach on all sides. We saw more evidence of police forces moving towards a shared agenda than drug agencies. The latter have been relatively slow to broaden the client-based focus of their work to incorporate a recognition of the wider interests of the community and of the impact of drug-related crime and drug dealing on the community.

1.7   The need to develop this shared agenda, and the gradual movement towards this, may be disrupted if Health and Local Authorities, as the purchasers of drug services, do not ensure that their purchasing strategies include both client-based and community safety elements. Consolidation and implementation of a shared agenda will require the establishment of organisational structures at the commissioning and service delivery levels and appropriate allocation of resources.

1.8   From our examination of policing, we have been convinced of the role that street level policing, such as the disruption of street dealing, has to play both in containing the extent of drug misuse and in reducing harm to the individual and the community. Street level policing needs the support of the community although identifying the different groups often involved and then recognising and reconciling their concerns is not without difficulty.

1.9   An important element of street level policing is the tactic of stop and search of individuals suspected of involvement in drug offences. A significant amount of activity involving drugs is concentrated in our inner cities, where ethnic minority populations are also heavily represented. In turn, this can result in apparently disproportionate numbers of ethnic minorities being stopped and searched compared with the general population. This emphasises the need for open and effective ethnic monitoring to ensure that street level policing activity is not discriminatory and that this can be demonstrated. Ethnic monitoring will not, by itself, eliminate discrimination but it will help to establish confidence amongst communities and increase police credibility.

1.10 Another aspect of drugs policing on which we heard much evidence concerns the problem of drug misuse associated with large scale music events such as festivals and raves. There is a limit to the extent to which enforcement and security action can be taken to prevent drug dealing at raves and other events. In our view, a harm reduction approach is appropriate here. The objective should be to encourage legal raves at the expense of the illegal events where the risks to health and public safety are considerable. This requires both the police and local authorities to devise licensing conditions which are consistent, reasonable and achievable for the organisers of such events and, from an early stage, consultation with the community on the selection of venues and organisational issues.

1.11 We are convinced of the value of police cautions in dealing positively with drug offending at street level. Increased street level policing will inevitably result in more petty drug offenders coming to notice for whom a caution is an appropriate and effective disposal. Our survey of police forces, however, showed a wide variety of policies and practice. While recognising that some variations will exist, we have accepted the arguments for the establishment of national guidelines for cautioning in drug cases. We have identified a number of factors which national guidelines could contain including the encouragement of taking a broad view of the offences and drug types which are amenable to cautioning.

1.12 An alternative option to prosecuting drug offenders on which we heard evidence, is the discontinuance of cases by the Crown Prosecution

Service (CPS). The criteria for discontinuance generally are set out in the Code for Crown Prosecutors, a public document known to defence solicitors and practitioners in the criminal justice system. However, our enquiries suggested that discontinuance is not well known either by drug agencies or the public; nor did we discern clearly articulated criteria for discontinuance in cases of drug offending. There is a need for greater liaison between the police and CPS and between the CPS and other agencies in establishing and operating public interest criteria in the field of drug offending.

1.13 A range of criteria should be used to assess the effectiveness of applying harm reduction principles to street level drugs enforcement. The development of local and street level strategies has not yet reached the stage where appropriate quantitative performance measures can be defined. As a first step we have framed some appropriate questions for H M Inspectors of Constabulary to ask on a regular basis during force inspections. We envisage performance measures will emerge from police responses to HMI's questions and from the implementation of recommendations on police reforms, such as those contained in the Home Office White Paper (June 1993).

1.14 The organisation of the police service is about to undergo a process of radical development and change. These developments are likely to give greater discretion to divisional commanders in responding to local conditions within strategic guidelines. We welcome the potential these developments have for local policing to develop in response to local community needs.

1.15 The evidence we heard about the medical care of drug misusers taken into police custody indicated wide variations in policies and treatment responses. We believe that there is much to be gained from guidelines to good practice in this area. They would bring advantages not only in improved standards of care but also in improved notification from this source and increased identification of drug misusers in custody. Good practice guidelines ought also to cover better liaison with other agencies and the training of practitioners in drug misuse.

1.16 Finally, we found throughout this phase of our work that we were hampered by the lack of research in this country into the effectiveness of different approaches to policing drug misuse. Consequently, it was necessary to look at the American experience to see what lessons had been learned. We recommend that more research be carried out in this field here and have been encouraged to learn of plans to fill the gap.

2. Drug Misusing Offenders and the Police Response

2.1 In Part 1 of our report we defined `drug misusing offenders' as those who came into contact with the criminal justice system either directly as a result of their misuse of controlled drugs or because their misuse of controlled drugs caused or contributed to their offences. We suggested that those who use the proceeds from property offences in order to finance their drug misuse were probably the largest group of offenders in our second category. We quoted some tentative estimates of the proportions of household burglaries, thefts from the person and shoplifting offences that may have been committed by regular heroin misusers in 1987 and noted that it was not known how many heroin users had been convicted of the offences. We also referred to the findings of a survey of a representative sample of the sentenced prison population in 1988 which found that appreciable minorities, particularly of women, were assessed as drug dependent. Most of the drug dependent prisoners had been convicted of property offences[1]. More recent research on regular cocaine or crack users[2] and regular amphetamine users[3] has shown that the majority admit to property offences and to selling drugs.

2.2 Given our initial terms of reference we were especially concerned in Part 1 of our report with the identification of those offenders whose misuse of controlled drugs had caused or contributed to their offences and the barriers to the self-disclosure of problem drug use. For this second report we

---

[1] Maden, A., Swinton, M. and Gunn, J. (1990) Women in prison and the use of illicit drugs before arrest. British Medical Journal, 301, pp 1133.
Maden, A., Swinton, M. and Gunn, J. (1992) A survey of pre-arrest drug use in sentenced prisoners. British Journal of Addiction, 87, pp 27-34.

[2] Dean, A. (1991) Cocaine and crime in Britain: an emerging perspective. In: Cocaine Today: its effects on the individual and society. Ed; Bruno, F. pp 246-253. Rome: UNICRI

[3] Klee, H. and Morris, J. (1993) Crime and drug misuse: economic and psychological aspects of the criminal activities of heroin and amphetamine injectors. Addiction Research (in press).

are also concerned with those whose contact with the criminal justice system is as a direct result of offences under the Misuse of Drugs Act 1971. We have not considered those people who engage in offences involving drugs without being drug misusers themselves, probably the majority of those convicted of unlawful production or import of controlled drugs[4]. As we noted earlier, unlawful import offences are investigated by HM Customs and Excise although the police may collaborate in some cases.

2.3   All drug misusers are at risk of being dealt with by the criminal justice system for offences under the Misuse of Drugs Act 1971, most usually for unlawful possession of a controlled drug. In Part 1 of our report we quoted Home Office estimates of between 35,000 and 90,000 regular heroin misusers and between 1 million and 1.5 million cannabis users in 1990 in the United Kingdom. These may well be under estimates. The findings of the survey of self-reported drug misuse conducted as part of the 1992 British Crime Survey, together with surveys of self-reported drug misuse in four areas in 1992 commissioned by the Home Office Central Drug Prevention Unit, will provide baseline estimates of the number of people in England and Wales who have used one or other of several drugs controlled under the Act. Of course, the number of people dealt with by the police and the courts for drug offences is as much a reflection of the enforcement efforts of the police, and HM Customs, as of the number of people misusing particular types of controlled drug. There can be no doubt that only a small minority of misusers are dealt with by the criminal justice system for drug offences.

2.4   Statistics of the number of persons found guilty by the courts or cautioned by the police, or dealt with by compounding by HM Customs, for offences involving controlled drugs in the United Kingdom are published annually by the Home Office. The number of people dealt with for drug offences (that is, offences under the Misuse of Drugs Act 1971 or under the

---

4   Dorn N., Murji, K. and South, N. (1992) Drug Traffickers. London: Routledge.

Green, P. (1991) Drug Couriers. London: Howard League.

Customs and Excise Act 1979 or for other offences involving controlled drugs) more than doubled between 1980 and 1992. In 1980 around 17,000 persons were found guilty by the courts or cautioned by the police, while in 1992 almost 49,000 persons were similarly dealt with or by compounding introduced by HM Customs and Excise in 1982.[5]

2.5   Since the 1970s the overwhelming majority of drug offences dealt with by the courts or the police have involved the unlawful possession of a controlled drug - 93 per cent in 1973, 82 per cent in 1980 and 90 per cent in 1992. Since the 1950s the majority of the offences have involved cannabis : about 50 per cent (of 169) in 1950, about 75 per cent (of almost 15,000) in 1973, about 85 per cent (of 17,000) in 1980 and about 85 per cent (of almost 49,000) in 1992[6]. The proportions of offences involving other drugs, or new versions of old drugs, have fluctuated according to fashions in youth culture. In the late 1960s and again in the mid-1980s amphetamines and LSD came to the fore, with MDMA (a hallucinogenic form of amphetamine known as Ecstasy) arriving on the scene in the late 1980s associated with the popularity of `raves'.

2.6   The response of the police to drug offenders has changed over the years: in 1980 only one percent of all those dealt with by the criminal justice system were cautioned, including 30 per cent of those aged under 17 but less than one per cent of those over 17. In 1992 50 per cent were cautioned, including almost 81 per cent of those aged under 17 and just under half of those aged over 17. There is, however, considerable variation between police forces in their cautioning policy, an issue which we discuss in detail later in this report.

---

[5]   If the same individual is found guilty, cautioned or dealt with by compounding for offences involving more than one controlled drug, once or several times during the year, they are counted on each occasion under each of the drugs involved.

[6]   Home Office (1951) Report to the United Nations on the working of the international treaties on narcotic drugs for 1950.
Home Office (1979) Statistics of the misuse of drugs United Kingdom 1977. London: Home Office
Home Office (1990,1991,1992) Statistics of Drug Seizures and Offenders dealt with, United Kingdom and area table. London: Home Office.

2.7   The national statistics show there is considerable variation, in terms both of the nature of the offence and the type of drug involved, in the proportions of offenders cautioned. In 1992 55 per cent of all those dealt with for unlawful possession of a controlled drug were cautioned compared with 8 per cent of all those dealt with for drug dealing offences (unlawful supply or possession with intent to supply unlawfully).

2.8   Offenders dealt with for unlawful possession of cannabis are the most likely to be cautioned. In 1992 over half (59 per cent) were cautioned compared with 10 per cent of those dealt with for offences of dealing in cannabis. The relatively high proportions of those dealt with in 1992 who were cautioned for unlawful possession of amphetamine (31 per cent) or LSD (28 per cent) or MDMA (Ecstasy) (28 per cent) probably reflects their youthfulness, and the popularity of `raves', although LSD and MDMA are Class A controlled drugs. Only around 14 per cent of those dealt with for unlawful possession of other Class A drugs - heroin, cocaine, methadone - were cautioned. One per cent of those dealt with for drug dealing offences involving cocaine or heroin were cautioned compared with three per cent of those whose offence involved methadone.

2.9   Against this background, the police and other enforcement agencies respond to drug offending, as with all other crime, in the context of the criminal justice system. The aims of our criminal justice system have been described[7] as to prevent and reduce crime, to dispense justice fairly, to protect the public, to punish the guilty and to acquit the innocent. The main aims of the police service were identified in the 1993 Police Reform White Paper:

(1)   to fight and prevent crime;

(2)   to uphold the law;

---

7   Home Secretary's foreword to Race and the Criminal Justice System published under Section 95 of the Criminal Justice Act 1991, September 1991.

(3)   to bring to justice those who break the law;

(4)   to protect, help and reassure the community;

(5)   in meeting those aims, to provide good value for money.

2.10 The police role in dealing with drug offences is complex, perhaps more so than with some other types of criminal activity. Although primarily concerned with reducing the supply of drugs the police are becoming increasingly involved in efforts to reduce the demand, as well as their other roles, for example, welfare and public education. The police enforcement response is largely derived from a Working Party of the Association of Chief Police Officers on drugs related crime which produced in 1985 the "Broome" report. This set out a structure for tackling drug crime on three levels:

I   A lower tier based at Divisional level where officers encountered drug misusers in the normal course of their duties.

II   Force drug squads targeting middle level dealers and co-ordinating force intelligence on drugs; and

III   Regional crime squads addressing major distributors and importers on a national and sometimes international level.

The efforts of police forces are supported by the Drugs Division of the National Criminal Intelligence Service, which was developed from the National Drugs Intelligence Unit in April 1992. Within the Broome structure, however, Chief Officers of Police are responsible for deciding on how drug misuse and trafficking should best be tackled within their own force areas and according to local conditions. We were warned, however, that this structure could not fully represent the dynamic situation which exists within the police service in responding to drug misuse and that significant changes in policing philosophy and management are contributing to this development. Several of the police officers who gave evidence left us with the impression that concerted action at the lower, Divisional level tier (I) had, until recently, been regarded as relatively unimportant.

2.11 Two basic policing philosophies were put to us:

- To enforce the law and

- to serve and protect.

Many police representatives with whom we spoke were increasingly coming to the view that drug misuse was not a problem which could be tackled by law enforcement alone. An alternative philosophy and strategy was appropriate. Conventional enforcement methods may succeed in suppressing street level activities - although less so in the most problematic inner city areas where only temporary relief from street drugs activity may be obtained and that at the risk of alienating sections of the local community. The "serve and protect" approach acknowledges the limitations of police in controlling crime in every form, and seeks to identify the most effective contribution that police can make to assist the community to deal with the problem of drug misuse. That contribution will include law enforcement; but, additionally, local knowledge and experience from working with a variety of other agencies and community groups with a view to influencing the problem in the long term.

2.12 Changes in policing philosophy are also being influenced by other factors. It is a time of almost unprecedented pressure on the police to review and revise their management, procedures and resourcing. The outcome of the Home Secretary's proposals for reform will have a profound effect on police forces. Much of this activity is being driven by assessments which have been produced by the Audit Commission on a wide range of police policies and practices. From these exercises a number of principles have emerged for developing the future structure and organisation of police forces. Those of special interest to us include:

- delegation of more responsibility to local police commanders, together with the provision of adequate information about performance and its financial consequences,

- proper and well structured local community consultation reinforced by regular surveys of customer reaction and public responses to policing; and

- a clear policy on policing styles, which reflects community demand.

We are also aware that changes are being driven internally by individual police forces and through the Association of Chief Police Officers' quality of service initiative.

2.13 As a result of these changes and the growing realisation that traditional enforcement methods are not always the only answer for dealing with what is a complex issue a new policing philosophy is evolving. It was suggested to us that the enforcement response should be integrated and taken forward on three fronts:

- supply

- demand

- multi-agency co-operation

We will return to each of these elements in more detail later in this Report.

2.14 The police response, however, also requires the setting of goals which are shared by other agencies with whom the police can co-operate. Since enforcement will not provide immediate success in tackling drug misuse, these goals should aim to reduce the incidence of misuse or reduce the harm which misuse causes to communities and individuals. The objectives in tackling drug misuse can be ranked in order of priority as follows:

- containment

- reduction

- elimination

The evidence we heard confirmed our view that some level of drug misuse is inevitable and that strategies devised solely with the objective of eliminating it were unrealistic and unattainable. Aiming at a reduction in the problem is in line with police targets for conventional crime but, given the complexities of drug misuse, is also seen as being some way off. Containment is generally regarded as the most realistic objective and we support this view. This does not mean passive acceptance of the present position but requires positive and concerted action.

2.15 We do not underestimate, however, the barriers that exist in the way of taking forward the approach outlined in 1.13 above. Within the police service, as in any organisation with a long tradition, the cultural change involved will be considerable. As a result of the changes in internal structure referred to earlier it will be local police commanders who will need convincing of the benefits that can flow from increased inter-agency co-operation. We have also been advised that the development of a common purpose between the police and other agencies will not be easy to achieve, given the differences in culture and philosophies of all those involved in the drug misuse arena. Inter-agency co-operation is, by its very nature, a two-way enterprise: it is naive to assume that only the police may require a change in philosophy. All agencies involved in the problem of drug misuse need to examine how they can co-operate with others in tackling the problem. The prospects for progress could also be hampered further by the lack of a structure in which multi agency working can develop and consolidate. Multi agency working challenges much of the practice and thinking of all concerned but it is worth investing in what we regard as an essential ingredient in tackling drug misuse.

3. Current Enforcement Strategies

3.1 We readily endorse the view that enforcement is a vital element in tackling drug misuse and can play a significant part in reducing both the supply of and demand for drugs. As has already been noted, the police enforcement role in this country is conducted at three levels - at the Divisional level in the normal course of police officers' duties, by force drug squads targeting middle-level dealers and by Regional Crime Squads addressing major distributors and traffickers. Drug enforcement strategies have been virtually unresearched in the UK and we were obliged to look at the American experience for lessons that could be learned in this field.

3.2 There has been a growing recognition in the USA that high level interception of drugs is limited in its cost effectiveness and must be supplemented by focused, street level strategies[1]. American based research suggests that attempts to apprehend the "Mr Bigs" of the drugs trade have usually been unsuccessful. A Mr Big could often continue to manage his operation from prison and, in any event, could be quickly replaced from the many people operating at a lower level in the drugs distribution system. Whilst apprehending Mr Big might serve the interests of justice, it would have little effect on the drugs trade in America. Transactions are now seen as the vulnerable part of the distribution network and interrupting deals as the easiest way to increase price and hence decrease demand. There is some supporting, if limited, evidence from UK studies for this theory[2].

---

[1] Moore, M. (1976) Buy and Bust: the effective regulation of an illicit market in heroin. Lexington: Heath.
Kleiman and Smith (1990) State and local drug enforcement: in search of a strategy. In: Drugs and Crime. Eds: Tonry, M. and Wilson, J.Q. London and Chicago: University of Chicago Press.
Moore, M. (1990) Supply reduction and law enforcement. In: Drugs and Crime. Eds: Tonry. M. and Wilson J.Q. London and Chicago: University of Chicago Press.
[2] Dorn, N. and Murji, K. (1992) Low level drug enforcement. International Journal of the Sociology of Law, 20, pp 159-172.

Street level operations

3.3   We were told that the difficulty of targeting those involved in the top end of the drugs trade in this country had led to an increased enthusiasm here for street level policing. This is aimed at drug deals taking place on the street, in other public places such as pubs, cafes, hotels and fast food outlets and also in private houses and flats. Essentially the objective is to disrupt deals by separating the buyer and seller. Disruption of this type of dealing can be achieved in a number of ways including:

- focusing on retailers to reduce the general availability of drugs

- focusing on buyers

- discouraging and inconveniencing users by increasing the time and costs involved in finding and purchasing drugs

Street level policing operations can be elaborate and resource intensive. They can also be dangerous as reports suggest that firearms and their use are becoming increasingly associated with some aspects of the drug trade, particularly where crack / cocaine is involved. We heard of operations mounted in areas where it had previously been difficult to tackle street dealing. These involved careful surveillance and logging all transactions over several weeks before carrying out simultaneous raids on the addresses of suspects. Simpler approaches involve arresting and cautioning all buyers as they left the area where deals had taken place. "Buy and bust" operations in which officers make a purchase from a street dealer and then make an arrest are also conducted by some forces. Other examples of street level policing of which we heard included the use of high profile uniformed police patrols and "flooding" areas where dealing is taking place with a police presence.

3.4   We must guard, however, against regarding street level policing as the ultimate solution. Apart from being resource intensive it can simply displace the market elsewhere, result in it taking place at different times, lead to diversification into different substances and develop more adept and security conscious dealers. **We recommend that a range of approaches, tailored to local circumstances and enforcement objectives, should be developed. We support the identification by the police of a set of street level strategies with likely outcomes on which local communities can be consulted and informed. This would enable the police to intervene more quickly in drug related incidents and in a more considered way.** Good working practices, which fully involve all levels of drug enforcement activity are clearly essential. We also recognise the need for Regional Crime Squads and others involved in national operations to be alive to local policing objectives.

Street level policing tactics - stop and search

3.5 We heard of several tactics being employed by the police at street level in order to deter and inconvenience buyers and sellers and generally to disrupt dealing. One approach favoured the intensive use of foot patrols, particularly to reclaim former 'no go' areas. This was said to be particularly effective in sensitive areas where more interventionist tactics could lead to public order incidents.

3.6 Stop and search is one of the most important and controversial methods of carrying out street level policing. It is not without its critics, particularly on the grounds that it may be discriminatory and can result in abuses. We have heard evidence, moreover, that in sensitive areas or during difficult times, stop and search may not be regarded as an option by the police. Powers to stop and search, and arrest without warrant, any person suspected of any offence involving controlled drugs are provided by the Misuse of Drugs Act 1971. A Code of Practice for the exercise of all statutory stop and search powers is provided by the Police and Criminal Evidence Act 1984 (PACE). In addition to its provisions, the Code also provides guidance notes on the exercise of these powers. The key features of the Code are:

- the requirement that reasonable grounds exist for suspicion that a person is in possession of a stolen or prohibited article (innocently or otherwise) before that person may be detained or searched

- the suspicion must have an objective basis (and not depend on personal factors, such as age, colour or previous conviction, either alone or in combination; nor on the basis of stereotyped images of certain persons or groups)

- that a person may only be detained for the purposes of a search; there is no power to stop or detain a person against his will in order to find grounds for a search

- an officer may question a person about the circumstances which gave rise to the suspicion, preparatory to the search. If as a result of questioning, the grounds for a search are eliminated, no search should take place.

- the cooperation of the person to be searched should be sought in every case; force may only be used as a last resort

- limits on the extent and thoroughness of the search, depending upon the circumstances of the search

- provisions for giving information to the person being searched and making a record of the search.

The Code also covers the use of statutory powers to search vehicles for controlled drugs.

3.7   Since the beginning of 1986, data on stops and searches for controlled drugs in England and Wales under the powers contained in the Misuse of Drugs Act 1971 have been collected to monitor the police powers introduced by PACE. In 1992, the police recorded 351,700 stops and searches under PACE; this represented a 16% increase on 1991 and was preceded by an 18% increase on 1990. The total number of stops and searches has more than trebled since 1986. Stops and searches for drugs increased by 14% and represented 35% of the total in 1992. This was a slightly larger increase than in 1991 (12%) but a smaller increase than in 1990 (24%) and 1989 (58%). The increase in stops and searches was not translated into arrests following stops and searches which increased by 5% in total and by 3% for drug offences. The total number of arrests made was 48,700. About 14% of all stops and searches resulted in an arrest with the corresponding figure for drugs at about 15% (18,195).

3.8   The increase in stops and searches and arrests recorded under PACE has been widespread across police forces. A number of reasons have been suggested for the increased use of PACE stop and search which include:

- increased availability of drugs

- a growing awareness of drug misuse on the part of the police

- pressure from the public to intervene

- its perceived effectiveness as a deterrent.

Others have suggested that the statistics do not reflect the whole picture because:

- the reason for stopping changes and the recorded reason may not be the original suspicion that led to the stop

- police have wider discretion to stop for drugs and may therefore cite drugs as the reason in borderline cases

- drugs may be found when searches are carried out for other reasons.

Wide differences exist between forces in the frequency with which stops and searches are carried out. In 1992, the Metropolitan Police carried out nearly 30 times as many stops and searches as were conducted in the Greater Manchester Police area despite having only four times the number of officers and three times the resident population to police. It is difficult to establish, however, whether such variations are due to differences in policing policy or in recording of practice.

3.9   We heard a number of concerns about the use of PACE stop and search as a police tactic. Some thought that as it allowed individual officers discretion to assess behaviour it was, therefore, inherently capable of abuse. It was also suggested that the tactic could be used as a means of controlling public order or even simply as a demonstration of police power.

3.10 **We regard stop and search as an essential element of street level policing providing there is quality control and that outcomes are properly monitored.** The emphasis must be on quality, not quantity. We heard of examples where following a number of civil actions being brought against the police more care was exercised in carrying out stops and searches. Fewer stops resulted but there was an increased arrest rate. Often the key is in surveillance carried out in advance of a stop and search operation. We are also convinced of the value of effective monitoring and that the data collected should be seen to be of interest to senior police management. Apart from ensuring that the tactic was not employed in a discriminatory manner the collection of additional data would also provide information about the epidemiology of drug misuse and assess the impact of police practices.

Community attitudes to policing drug misuse

3.11 We have referred in chapter 1 to developments in policing philosophy, organisation and management and noted the trend towards delegation of more responsibility to local police commanders and the establishment of effective local community consultation backed up by regular surveys of "customer" reaction. Increasingly police forces are breaking away from an impersonal fire brigade style to continuous policing by teams or individual officers of neighbourhoods and communities. This effectively ties the police more tightly into local communities.

3.12 We recognise the need for the police to consult and listen to the views of local communities before designing appropriate strategies to deal with drug misuse - but in itself this process can be problematic. Communities are often complex structures made up of disparate groups of people with different agendas. Some consultative committee groups will regard subtle, low key police operations as inaction and campaign for more police activity. On the other hand, operations to target dealers may result in excessive policing with the police rather than drugs being viewed as the problem. **There is a need for local initiatives to take account of local differences and for the police to get over to communities the various options available to the police and the reasons for adopting particular strategies.**

Law Enforcement and Cannabis

3.13 Police action in response to cannabis possession and dealing can result in clashes with communities, particularly ethnic groups in inner cities. One community representative from an area with a high rate of unemployment told us that police targeting of young, unemployed Afro-Caribbean male cannabis street dealers was regarded as unfair, particularly as cannabis dealing was said to be the only source of income for this group. Many cannabis users in such communities were also described as upright and otherwise law abiding and not deserving of police attention in this way.

3.14 The public are said to be more concerned with drugs such as heroin and cocaine, needles in the street and the activities of dealers than with casual cannabis misuse. It was suggested to us that as cannabis was widely used there was a case for targeting more harmful drugs instead and the dealers who sold them. A contrary view suggested poly drug dealing made it impossible for the police to target specific drugs in this way. The fact remains that cannabis is illegal and the police are obliged to enforce the law in respect of the drug. With the availability and use of cannabis so widespread it is inevitable that street level police activity will, whatever its objectives, also result in a high level of seizures and arrests for cannabis and this will continue to be a rubbing point between the police and some people within ethnic communities.

4. A Harm Reduction Approach: Limiting Damage to the Community

4.1   We referred in Chapter 1 to the growing recognition that containment rather than elimination of drug misuse is the more realistic objective. Increasingly this is leading a growing number of police forces to adopt harm reduction principles in developing their enforcement and prevention strategies. Harm reduction principles have been largely developed in the context of health education and treatment services, particularly in the context of HIV/AIDS, where the focus has been primarily on the individual. The principles of harm reduction also have an application to the criminal justice system, and particularly to policing. Here the primary focus shifts to the community when the approach is sometimes described as community damage limitation, a term which may command wider understanding. Whether called harm reduction or community damage limitation, the objectives are similar : reducing the harm caused by drug misuse to the community and to the individual. We have examined harm reduction in the policing context and the implications of adopting such principles for all those involved.

4.2   From the evidence we have heard we have been impressed by the benefits for the community and for the individual to be gained from the harm reduction approach to enforcement against drugs misuse. **We recommend the wider adoption of harm reduction principles in developing enforcement strategies.**

4.3   Harm reduction has a relatively precise meaning in circles concerned with drug misuse. It is a term applied to an intervention which recognises that, for the foreseeable future, some people will misuse drugs and it therefore seeks to minimise the harm which their misuse causes to themselves or others. This approach has been developed extensively following publication of our report "AIDS and Drug Misuse - Part One" in which we proposed a hierarchy of goals:

[i]   becoming drug free
[ii]   switching from injecting to oral use
[iii] avoiding sharing equipment

This hierarchy has been further developed in our third report on AIDS and Drug Misuse to encompass:

[i]   facilitating cessation of drug use
[ii]   discouraging new recruitment into experimentation with drugs
[iii] discouraging regular drug use among experimental drug users
[iv]   discouraging drug injecting among potential injectors
[v]   promoting early retirement from injecting among current injectors
[vi]   encouraging regular injectors to switch to safer practices such as oral drug use
[vii] ensuring that all drug users have access to advice on safer sexual practices and safer injecting practices, as well as access to sterile injecting equipment and information about cleaning injecting equipment properly.

In practice this approach has resulted in the development of a variety of interventions which seek to influence different levels of drug misuse: these include outreach work, needle and syringe exchange, prescribing services, local prevention campaigns, etc. We believe that a similar hierarchy of goals could be applied to the policing context.

Harm Reduction in the Policing Context

4.4   In the policing context, harm reduction implies a recognition that under current circumstances enforcement of the laws against drug misuse cannot eliminate misuse but that it can have an effect on the level of harm to individuals and to society caused by misuse. **We recommend that an enforcement strategy which aims to limit the harm to individuals and damage to the community from drug misuse** should have the following characteristics:

[i] Where choices have to be made between enforcement operations against different kinds of drugs, the drug which causes most harm should be the principal target. It will not always be possible for policing strategies to target individual drugs, given the extent of polydrug misuse, but the enforcement process can take this into account.

[ii] If possible, where choices have to be made between enforcement operations, priority should be given to early intervention to eliminate drug dealing sites, particularly new locations, before these have the chance to establish and advertise themselves.

[iii] Enforcement should support the efforts of other agencies working to reduce the harm caused by drug misuse.

[iv] A recognition that harm reduction has a part to play in returning areas to normality through improvements to the environment, such as better street lighting, public buildings and amenities.

4.5 Harm reduction principles are not incompatible with vigorous street policing, indeed in many circumstances they actually require it, and enforcement agencies which follow policies based on these principles are more likely to be accused of abuse of civil liberties than of taking a soft option. Neither is harm reduction limited to individual misusers and their immediate circle. Concentration on the needs of misusers could exclude consideration of the wider community who are also harmed by drug misuse. In this context, the wider community's interests would certainly be served by vigorous, focused, street level enforcement. These interests include reducing the fear of drug related crime to finance misuse, crime associated with street dealing and the threat to public health (eg HIV/AIDS). But the outcome of street level enforcement strategies for the community needs to be monitored closely. If, for example, a crackdown on dealing in a public place leads to dealers switching their business operations to a private house (and drug availability and consumption remain undiminished) this may be regarded as a failure in enforcement terms. But the other outcome may be to restore a public amenity for the benefit of the wider community in which case the police should be given the credit. **We recommend that a range of criteria should be adopted to judge the effectiveness of applying harm reduction principles to street level drug enforcement.**

4.6   The effectiveness of the harm reduction approach will depend not only on the police establishing effective links with the community but also on good interagency co-operation. We have heard of many examples of valuable interagency co-operation including the mutual training of police and drug services' personnel and schools/parents groups, arrest referral schemes and joint publicity and prevention campaigns. There is the suspicion, however, that this co-operation is largely cosmetic and results either from the agencies concerned being forced together by extreme circumstances or depends for its cohesion on the drive and personality of a few individuals. At the heart of this concern is the question of whether enforcement agencies and drug services do indeed have a shared agenda in tackling drug misuse. Both are influenced by different philosophies with the police role being based on concepts such as the law and good of the community whereas drug services focus almost exclusively on minimising harm to their clients and, beyond that, improving their quality of life. These differences can create professional and ethical tensions between the agencies concerned which in turn hamper effective working relationships.

4.7   This picture is, however, over simplistic. Drug services, like the rest of society, depend on the maintenance of public order and the effective operation of the rule of law. Similarly, in pursuit of their enforcement role, the police can exercise wide discretion in the public interest to take account of the balance of cost and benefit to the individual and society. Where harm minimisation to the individual is not in conflict with the police role of promoting the common good then both the practice and theory of policing allow the exercise of discretion so that individuals can be diverted from the criminal justice system. It may be, therefore, that there are more points of common interest between police and drugs services than might otherwise be supposed.

4.8   As we have described earlier, there are two complementary policing philosophies - to enforce the law; to serve and protect. Similarly, there are two complementary drug service philosophies - to reduce the risk of an individual engaging in drug misuse; to reduce the harm associated with drug misuse. There has, however, been a pressure on drug services to concentrate the majority of their attention on responding to the needs of injecting drug misusers. This has limited the opportunities for developing a shared agenda with the police or with other agencies which have an interest in reducing the wider harm arising from drug misuse.

4.9   We saw more evidence of police forces having a greater readiness to move towards a shared agenda than drug agencies. The latter have been relatively slow to broaden the client-based focus of their work to incorporate a recognition of the wider interests of the community and of the impact of drug-related crime and drug dealing on the community. At the same time, we recognise that police culture still attaches higher status to the crime control role over the prevention/ welfare activities in multi-agency working. Shifting this balance will entail a major cultural change and we heard examples of problems arising as a result of police policies being interpreted differently by those responsible for their delivery on the ground. There are signs, however, of police forces increasingly taking the initiative in pursuit of partnership. This has often been pursued in the face of suspicion of the motives of the police and on occasions, open hostility.

4.10　We have already referred to examples of multi-agency co-operation with harm reduction as an underlying principle. As we have noted, there are many examples of co-operation between police forces and drug agencies. It seems to us that there is now an onus on these agencies to take a broader view and develop their focus to incorporate community safety as well as care of the individual drug misuser. Much of the present co-operation has been concerned with separate agreements on particular approaches, for instance arrest referral schemes, in the absence of a broader strategy of community damage limitation. The need now is for the development of common purpose and a shared agenda. This will require a change of approach from the drug services as well as from the police. Without this change, community based strategies will be difficult, if not impossible to implement.

4.11　The starting point of a shared agenda must be a common understanding of the philosophies underlying the work of the different agencies. As we have noted, there is no inherent incompatibility between the philosophies but concentration on particular strategies can lead to conflict. Thus, the police service in responding to community demands for action against street drug activity may undermine a drugs service in its effort to attract as many drug misusers as possible into treatment. A shared agenda would recognise the common purpose of all the agencies involved as being to minimise the harm caused by drug misuse to the individual in so far as this is compatible with community safety and the public interest.

4.12　At a strategic planning level, there would then be the need for agreement on the size and nature of the problem to be addressed. Drug services will need to recognise that community safety is a legitimate area of concern and for the police service, recognition that limiting the spread of HIV infection is an appropriate priority and that abstinence may be unattainable in the short term.

4.13 The need to develop this shared agenda, and the gradual movement towards this, may be disrupted if Health and Local Authorities, as the commissioners and purchasers of drug services, do not ensure that their purchasing strategies incorporate both client-based and community safety elements.

4.14 The barriers to forging successful alliances between all the agencies involved exist at both strategic planning and operational levels. Overcoming them will require action to establish effective planning and operational structures, funding and identification of arbitration procedures and appropriate sanctions and levers to ensure compliance with the agreed common purpose. We examine these issues in more detail in the next chapter on multi-agency working.

5. Multi-Agency Working

5.1   We referred in the previous chapter to the increasing adoption by the police of harm reduction principles in policing drug misuse and how this required the establishment of effective links with the community as well as good inter-agency co-operation. While few would disagree that multi-agency co-operation is a laudable principle, we have found that even after a brief consideration of the issues a number of problems can be identified which have the potential to hinder the development and maintenance of an effective alliance between the police, other agencies and the community in tackling drug misuse.

5.2   As a concept, the police in partnership with other agencies is well established. For more than a decade a partnership approach has been adopted in the field of crime prevention as well as in dealing with child abuse and racial harassment. This involves the Government, police, local authorities, probation and other agencies, along with the private sector in working together to devise activities aimed at preventing crime and reducing the fear of crime. A review of the arrangements, "Partnership in Crime Prevention" published in 1990, outlined progress and lessons learned in building up partnerships and included examples of good practice. Since then, progress on local partnerships has accelerated, with an emphasis on community safety. [1]   At the same time, Government initiatives have enabled the development of activities aimed at particular problems or localities.

5.3   An example of this latter approach applied to the drugs scene is the Home Office Drug Prevention Initiative. Launched in October 1989 as a partnership between Government and the community to promote the prevention of drug misuse, the aim of the Initiative is to ensure that communities are properly informed, encouraged and supported in their resistance against drug misuse. It seeks the active participation of interested

---

[1]   Local Authorities and the Police: Working in Partnership. ALA, AMA, LBA. London, 1993
Community Safety: Local Perspectives. AMA, LGDF. London, 1993

local people and professional, statutory and voluntary organisations. The Initiative is targeted at preventing people who have never used drugs, or have used them experimentally, from becoming or continuing as misusers. It seeks to achieve this by building on and enhancing existing work in education and health by mobilising local communities to initiate, promote and sustain drugs prevention activity. Local drugs prevention teams have been established in twenty areas around Great Britain. Each team is guided by a local advisory group comprising representatives from a wide range of statutory and voluntary agencies, including the police, and from other groups and individuals in the local community. This group advises the team on local drugs problems and on existing services, contributes to and agrees the team's programme of work, and considers and agrees applications for grant aid.

5.4 Experience of the Crime Prevention Partnership, the Drugs Prevention Initiative and the existing District Drugs Advisory Committees serves to illustrate the difficulties of achieving effective multi-agency co-operation on drug misuse. Several points have emerged which appear to us to be important factors in promoting effective joint action to tackle problems arising from drug misuse.

5.5 We have already noted the need for drug services to incorporate community safety issues into their work and for police to develop a harm reduction approach to policing drug misuse. These developments, however, need to be within an overall strategy appropriate to local circumstances. Many community safety strategies, which have been developed jointly by the police and local authorities, have recognised that tackling problems associated with drug misuse is an important element of that overall strategy. From the evidence we have received, local authorities have not been adequately involved in the development of local drug misuse strategies, which have often been led by health authorities and service providers. Given the wide range of responsibilities vested in local authorities and the powers conferred on them by statute, recognition of their essential role is vital if effective joint action on drug misuse is to be promoted.

5.6   To facilitate the developments which we consider desirable, we have already referred to the need to establish structures within which different agencies can operate in partnership effectively. Loose coalitions, without formal structures or lines of accountability, are unlikely to last much beyond the official impetus provided by good intentions. Experience from crime prevention and community safety partnerships favours the devising of structures suited to local circumstances. These have proved effective in supporting and encouraging local efforts.

5.7   We have heard of examples of inter-agency co-operation and have received evidence from a number of these. A central issue is the extent to which the agencies can establish a common purpose. Considerable effort requires to be invested in this in order that the legitimate concerns and interests of the participating agencies are adequately addressed. Where this has been done, it has been possible to develop agreements, variously described as strategy statements or charters, to which the most senior decision making level in each participating agency has been able to commit the organisation.

5.8   First, therefore, there is a need to establish a local partnership in which all the relevant agencies can be represented focused on the common purpose we have proposed in Chapter Three. It is, in our view, essential that such a local partnership is as concerned with community interests and safety as it is with prevention of drug misuse and the treatment and rehabilitation of drug misusers. The purpose of such a partnership should be primarily to identify strategic objectives in responding to drug misuse and the shared agenda between agencies which need to be active participants in developing and implementing actions in support of the common purpose and strategic objectives. Such a partnership should also be responsible for monitoring progress and revising objectives in the light of changing circumstances. It has been found that local government areas can provide an appropriate basis for drawing together interested parties.

5.9   Second, there is a need to invest in the partnership. The cultural changes which may be required and the development of trust between the agencies necessary to implement effective action cannot readily be achieved without dedicated resources. This will require employers to designate responsible staff for the partnership and to provide the time for the partnership to be developed.

5.10   At the operational level, there is a need for agencies to develop local alliances to plan and implement specific programmes of action. We use the word alliance deliberately, with its connotation of a temporary association where the common object and the mutual benefit is stated and defines what is affected by the agreement. It allows for considerable differences between allies in those parts of their work which have no relevance to the common object.

5.11   We have already referred in the previous chapter to police involvement in the development of practical schemes with local authorities to improve the environment in which drug crime takes place as a way of reducing the harm to the community and returning the area to normality. We heard of one initiative whereby a road in which drug dealing had been carried out was altered from a cul-de-sac to a thoroughfare. This had reduced criminal activity considerably. Street lighting had also been improved and shop rents reduced to attract small businesses into the area. These and other measures to uplift the environment had increased civic pride and the morale of local residents. Another example we learned about was a planned anti-drug operation involving the police, local authority, the community and local drug services. The police following surveillance were able to identify key drug dealing sites. The local authority, in addition to environmental improvements and the development of improved security measures in the area, used its powers to close a hotel used for drug dealing and to restrict licences for fast-food outlets. The drug services were available to provide support and access to treatment to drug misusers in the area. As well as more complex alliances, other examples of specific alliances might be: the development of arrest referral schemes; the provision of drug service information cards to those cautioned for a drug related offence; an agreement on intelligence sharing enabling both drug service provision and policing to be most effectively targeted; and, mutual training to improve knowledge and understanding and to promote confidence between personnel in the different services.

5.12 These examples underline the importance of undertaking an audit of existing partnerships to tackle community safety and the problems associated with drug misuse. The value of partnership is in enhancing and building upon existing work, adjusting activities to be mutually supportive and drawing on the benefits of the powers and skills the members of the partnership can bring in support of the common purpose. In this, the local authority can make a very considerable contribution.

5.13 The evidence we have received has convinced us of the need to involve the local media in support of the common purpose, the partnership and the strategic objectives. The media is often the voice through which the local community is able to express its concerns and campaigns for action. If it is not co-opted into the partnership it may undermine the careful planning and development of effective action, which will take time, by demands for more immediate but less effective reaction. Where it has been co-opted into the partnership and time has been taken to explain the reasons for particular courses of action, this can complement consultation with the local community and strengthen the partnership.

5.14 The establishment of effective structures also raises the question of securing adequate resourcing of activities. There has been an increasing move towards Health and Local Authorities and the Probation Service becoming purchasers as well as providers of services. Proposed changes for the police service provide a basis for resources to be targeted in line with local needs and priorities. Each of these agencies involved will have its own sources of funding with which to finance core responsibilities and programmes. Agencies should ensure that their commissioning and purchasing strategies support and progress the common purpose and strategic objectives. In particular, they should recognise that the promotion of community safety is a legitimate and necessary element in the response to drug misuse.

5.15 Difficulties arise when new projects or programmes cut across traditional boundaries and responsibilities and require either new money or pooling of existing resources. The adoption of a wider welfare role by the police cannot readily be funded from existing sources. Likewise moves by drug agencies to extend their work into communities, as well as for individuals, could not easily be met from their present income. Commissioners and purchasers of services will need to explore between themselves how they might most effectively utilise their available resources and assist in the securing of additional resources to develop further activities. Each agency should also include their plans for progressing the strategic objectives in their relevant documents, for instance, the Community Care Plan, local police strategies, and the like.

5.16 Another factor in the promotion of partnership is the availability of information. An effective response to drug misuse must be based on accurate and up to date information. All the agencies involved have something to contribute in this respect. For example, the police have crime statistics for the area concerned together with other information that has been gathered in the course of policing drug misuse; drugs services have information obtained from their own perspective on the drugs scene as well as that obtained from clients; local authorities have information obtained from their various departments including environmental health, housing, social services as well as from community, residents and tenants associations. Some of these sources guard their information, quite properly in some instances when, for example, the police need to avoid compromising operations against criminal activity or, in the case of drugs services, to protect client confidentiality. Pooling information will be an important element in promoting partnership and the extent to which it is achieved will be a measure of the soundness of the co-operation and trust which is established. As an example, we considered the possibility of the police sharing intelligence about the appearance of new drugs on the scene, particularly where forensic analysis of the drug concerned suggested it would be desirable for drug agencies to alert potential misusers to a harmful formulation. We were encouraged by the readiness to which consideration is being given to making available information of this sort. At a national level, this information is too general to have operational value. At the local level, however, it could allow early intervention which could limit harm to drug misusers, disrupt the establishment of drug dealing in a new area or provide a focus for intensified work to make contact with drug misusers not presently in contact with services.

5.17 As we have indicated, developments along the lines which we have proposed will not be easy and will take time. We believe that there is an appropriate role for the different inspectorates, Constabulary, Social Services, Probation and Education to monitor and report on progress in establishing partnerships and alliances and in implementing planned programmes of activity. Regional Health Authorities, in monitoring and reviewing health authority planning and purchasing could similarly review arrangements for partnership and the extent to which community safety has been included as an element in the purchasing and delivery of, for instance, drug services and health promotion. We propose later in this report key areas which could be monitored by HM Inspectorate of Constabulary. Other inspectorates could develop complementary areas in their own areas of competence. There is also a role for the NHS Drugs Advisory Service to ensure that its peer review of responses to drug problems in a Health Authority area includes examination of partnership arrangements and the development of local alliances in support of a common purpose and agreed strategic objectives.

5.18 Effective drugs education in schools also requires good inter-agency co-operation within a recognised framework. This subject has been considered in detail by the 1993 report 'Drugs Education in Schools: The Need For New Impetus' by the Advisory Council on the Misuse of Drugs. We heard two view of the police role. The first of these envisages the police being actively involved in the delivery of drugs education in the classroom. This often results from the police being called in to take an active role because schools are unsure about how to tackle the issue. The second approach, which we endorse, is that drugs education in the classroom is the responsibility of teachers. Nevertheless, we saw evidence of effective work being performed by the police in education, based on multi-agency co-operation. We endorse the view of the "Drugs Education in Schools" report that the police are particularly well placed to ensure that legal issues and police practice are understood by parents, teachers and pupils alike.

5.19 In promoting effective joint action to tackle the problems associated with drug misuse, we recommend:

- **The establishment of a common purpose between all the agencies involved.**

- **Recognition of the essential role of local authorities.**

- **The development of effective structures under which agencies can co-operate and on which they are represented, in order to identify strategic objectives, and monitor progress.**

- **Investment in the partnership through the designation of responsible staff and the provision of adequate time for them to develop it.**

- **The development within these partnership arrangements of local alliances to plan and implement specific programmes of action.**

- Engaging the local media in the efforts being made.

- Adequate resourcing of these activities by the authorities which commission and purchase services and, in particular, the recognition by those authorities that the promotion of community safety is a legitimate and necessary element of the response to drug misuse.

 The sharing of information by all the partners.

- Regular monitoring and reporting on progress in establishing partnerships and alliances by the inspecting arms of the relevant agencies, including police, health and social services inspectorates.

6. Policing Youth Culture

6.1   One of the greatest concerns about drug misuse is the danger it poses for the young. Children and young people are seen to be at particular risk due to their natural urge to experiment, their inexperience and the consequences of peer pressure. Fears are expressed for the health of young people who misuse drugs and the deaths that occur receive considerable media publicity. Over the past thirty years or so drug misuse by the young has been viewed mainly in the context of youth culture and popular music together with the recreational use of drugs to enhance the experience of leisure activities. While many aspects of youth culture are not problematic the police can be presented with particular problems in enforcing the law, maintaining order and protecting persons and property.

6.2   Developments in youth culture and trends in popular music have been accompanied by fashions in drugs. For example, in the late 1950's and 1960's, with the development of beat and hippy counter cultures, cannabis and LSD were used by some young people as a means of seeking self discovery and self expression and as a symbol of the rejection of the materialist values of the affluent society and the work ethic [1]. Further trends have been observed over the years. One recent development saw a considerable increase in the use of MDMA (Ecstasy) and LSD which became closely associated with the rave scene.

6.3   Various theories have addressed whether raving is simply another leisure activity or if it has some deep, underlying political or cultural thrust. Some commentators view raving as a routine development of youthful hedonism and risk taking[2]. Others believe that raving constitutes an attempt by working class youth to escape from forms of leisure sanctioned by the State by organising their own leisure activities at their own times and sites[3]. The scene continues to mutate with, as we report,

---

[1] Young, J. (1971) The Drug Takers. London: Paladin.
[2] Plant, M. & Plant, M. (1992) Risk takers. London: Tavistock/Routledge.
[3] Newcombe, R. (1992) A researcher reports from the rave. Druglink, 7, pp 14-15.

the development of smaller scale events in church halls and private houses. Another example of this diversification concerns the emergence of the "Bhangra" music and dance scene. This started to develop in the 1980's as an Asian version of British youth culture using traditional Indian sub-continent music adapted to developments in western pop music. Originally, events took place on week day afternoons to avoid parental curfews. In recent years weekend night dance venues have developed, often attracting 800-1000 young people, largely of Asian descent. The Bhangra scene shares some of the characteristics of the rave scene such as musical styles, the movement of venues from one urban location to another and a variety of drug preferences. More generally, raves are held at a variety of venues from established clubs and other properly licensed premises to disused factories and warehouses. At these events distinctive high volume music accompanies prolonged energetic dancing of the ravers.

6.4   Ecstasy is the drug most closely associated by the public with the rave scene and receives most media attention. Given the fashions and variety of drugs involved over the years, however, we believe it is potentially misleading to concentrate on drug types in considering the policing of youth culture. The issues for the police here are the drug trade associated with such events, together with health, safety and security aspects connected with the structure, facilities and management of venues.

6.5   There is a limit to the extent to which enforcement and security action can be taken to prevent drug dealing at such events. Even the most vigilant action by door staff cannot prevent drugs from being smuggled into raves, particularly as staff cannot legally conduct strip or intimate body searches, and may encourage drug taking before entering the venue. In any case, it is claimed that door and other security staff are frequently involved in the drug dealing that takes place and we comment later in this chapter on the need for regulating and training such staff.

6.6   The health and safety hazards connected with the rave scene have been well publicised. There have been a number of deaths associated with the use of Ecstasy. Published statistics show that at least fourteen deaths attributed to Ecstasy or similar drugs were registered by 1991 and there have been press reports of a number of more recent deaths apparently from Ecstasy use which may not yet have been reflected in official statistics. The pharmacological actions of Ecstasy on the brain are such as to disturb the control of body temperature. In addition, some misusers may have medical conditions which make them especially susceptible to the effects of Ecstasy. The problem of drug misuse at raves is worsened by the adulteration of substances and the conditions at venues. Raves tend to be crowded and hot which interferes with heat loss from the body. The dancing of users may be extremely vigorous and prolonged and this extensive physical activity also helps to raise body temperature. These factors can result in severe increases in body temperatures and dehydration levels which are thought to have been the causes of the reported deaths. It is also thought that some individuals are inherently more vulnerable to the effects of the drug. Lack of drinking water and/or high prices charged for water and soft drinks which occur particularly at the illegal or poorly organised raves together with poor or non-existent facilities for cooling off add significantly to the health risks.

6.7   The tragic deaths that have occurred from using Ecstasy at raves have tended to overshadow serious concerns expressed by police officers and others at the potential for far greater loss of life at raves resulting from a crowd disaster. We were told that at many illegal raves, and some legal ones, the number of people present far exceeds the safe capacity of the venue. Illegal raves are often held in disused industrial premises without fire equipment, ventilation or safety lighting. Fire escapes may be blocked and the parked cars of ravers in unsuitable settings would prevent emergency service responding effectively in the event of an incident. Crowds packed into unsuitable premises or sites also inhibit direct police action as this could create a panic with disastrous consequences. These factors have led us to conclude that a harm reduction approach to the rave scene is the most

42

appropriate course of action. Faced with the dilemma of taking enforcement action or preserving public safety we endorse the view we heard from some police officers who advocated the latter option. Overall, the objective should be to encourage well managed legal raves at the expense of the illegal events where the risk to health and public safety are considerable.

Licensing Conditions

6.8   Encouraging legal raves requires both the police and local authorities to devise licensing conditions which are consistent, reasonable and achievable for the organizers of such events and, from an early stage, consultation with the community on the selection of venues and organizational issues. Under present legislation, it is an offence to organize events involving public music and dancing without a licence obtained from the local authority in advance. The purpose of the licensing regime for such events is to ensure adequate standards of safety and hygiene and to minimise any nuisance to the immediate neighbourhood. In considering applications for the grant or renewal of entertainment licences the local authority will consider the views of the police and fire authority concerned.

6.9   Local authorities have very wide discretion over whether or not to grant entertainment licences and to attach terms and conditions to any licence granted. The growth of acid house parties and raves in the late 80's led the Government to take action to deter the organization of illegal events by increasing the penalties for infringement of the entertainment licensing laws. A maximum fine of £20,000, imprisonment for up to six months, or both can be imposed under the Entertainment (Increased Penalties) Act 1990. In addition, Magistrates were given the power to make confiscation orders in respect of the profits made from such events. We are also aware of Government plans to provide new powers to enable the police to direct gatherings of ten or more people to leave a site where the police believe that a rave will take place and that a local community will suffer distress as a result. It is further proposed that failure to heed such a direction will be made a criminal offence.

6.10   We believe there are dangers in over-regulation and in resorting to the criminal law which may well lead to conflict between young people and the authorities. **We recommend that the organisation of more legal raves be encouraged by local authorities exercising maximum discretion in the granting of licences and by involving responsible organisers of raves in the process.** Raves at established venues such as nightclubs are, of course, much easier to regulate. Here we have heard examples of multi agency co-operation taking place to provide a healthy and safe environment for ravers. We have been impressed by the code of standards drawn up by Manchester City Council and Lifeline, a voluntary drug agency, to be adopted by dance parties and clubs in the city. The code is voluntary but is monitored by the Council and refusal to comply could result in the withdrawal or refusal of an entertainment licence. We have also been informed that the Local Government Drugs Forum, with the support of the Home Office Drugs Prevention Initiative, is similarly intending to encourage good practice in this area. Current discussions are hoping to involve environmental health officers in the development of guidelines linked to the entertainment licensing system. **We recommend that the criteria for the granting of licences for raves and other such events by local authorities should include:**

- **availability of free cold water**

- **provision of rest facilities in a cool environment**

- **monitoring of temperature and air quality**

- **provision of information and advice on drugs**

- **compliance with a regulatory scheme for the selection, training and management of door staff**

6.11   We do not underestimate, however, the largely negative attitude with which raves and open air festivals are regarded by the general public. This is undoubtedly reflected in the proposals we referred to earlier to extend the law dealing with large-scale illegal raves. We are aware that the police and licensing authorities often come under considerable pressure from local communities to prevent large-scale music events from taking place. Networks do exist, however, to assist local authorities, particularly those with little experience of licensing large-scale music events. For example, Festival Welfare Services can act as negotiators with the promoters of such events to ensure that minimum standards of public safety and security are in place. Advice can also be provided on ways to ensure the minimum of disruption to the local community.

Door Staff

6.12   Door staff are usually employed to regulate persons entering a venue and to supervise the security and behaviour of those inside. We have already referred to the part that many door and security staff are said to play in the drug trade associated with raves and other large scale music events, such as open air festivals. A survey conducted by the Home Office several years ago found significant problems in several parts of the country. This showed that around 60% of police force areas had been experiencing problems of sufficient magnitude with door supervisors to have prompted the setting up of local regulatory schemes or to plan to set up such schemes. The serious problems included incidents of violence, intimidation and, in about 20% of cases, drug dealing.

6.13   Regulatory schemes established by local authorities and representatives of the entertainment industry involve:

- taking up character references and clearing appointments with the police and local authority

- ensuring individual door supervisors can be identified and traced

- training.

We also heard of a security charter drawn up by Festival Welfare Services, in consultation with the police, security firms and others, which sets out similar provisions in respect of open air festivals.

6.14 Compliance with a regulatory scheme is now often a condition for grant or renewal of an entertainment licence. The Home Office has been monitoring the operation of a number of these schemes and consideration is currently being given to proposals to put the regulation of door staff on a statutory basis. We make no recommendation on the question of statutory versus voluntary regulation but support the growing trend to ensure that only fit and proper persons are employed for these duties and that adequate management systems are in place to supervise staff effectively.

6.15 Clearly it is not possible for door staff to prevent all drugs from being smuggled into a venue or identify everyone who has taken drugs beforehand. However, selecting and training the door staff concerned should influence the level of drug misuse.

Misuse of Drugs Act 1971 - Section 8

6.16 In considering the options for police enforcement action at raves the issue of possible legislative changes has been raised. Section 8 of the Misuse of Drugs Act 1971 makes it an offence for occupiers or managers of premises to knowingly permit:

(a)   the production of a controlled drug

(b)   supplying or attempting to supply a controlled drug

(c)   preparing opium for smoking

(d)   the smoking of cannabis, cannabis resin or opium on their premises.

The suggestion has been made that Section 8(d) and possibly 8(c) should be amended to cover a wide range of, or all, controlled drugs. The present limited list of drugs specified in the section was said to be anomalous given the wide variety of drugs currently being misused. Extending the range to all controlled drugs would give the police powers, and provide deterrents, for tackling drug dealing at raves, clubs and pubs in drugs not currently specified in the Act.

6.17 We heard of widespread support amongst police forces for an extension to the provision. The fears that parents could be liable for drug taking by their children at home were said to be unfounded. Counter arguments, however, have been put including the legal difficulties of proving that an offence had taken place. The matter was still under consideration as this Report was being prepared. Extension of Section 8(d) may improve some aspects of the police drugs enforcement response but the issue is a delicate one which will require careful assessment.

7. Cautioning

7.1   We are convinced of the value of police cautions in dealing positively with drug offenders. Cautioning diverts petty offenders from the courts system and is undoubtedly cost effective in terms of police time and that of other agencies in the criminal justice system. We have already noted in Chapter 2 that since 1980 the police have increasingly dealt with drug offenders by cautioning, with just over a half of all drug offenders being cautioned in 1992. Increased street level policing will inevitably result in more petty offenders coming to notice for whom a caution is an appropriate and effective disposal.

7.2   In England and Wales the police may formally caution an arrested offender instead of initiating prosecution by the Crown Prosecution Service. The procedure is not used in Scotland. Although the practice of formal cautioning has statutory recognition, it is nowhere defined in legislation and is essentially an administrative act based on the discretion the police have in whether or not to prosecute suspected offenders.

7.3   In 1985 and 1990 the Home Office issued Circulars on cautioning to all Chief Officers of Police with the aim of promoting more effective and nationally consistent practice. The 1990 Circular (Home Office 59/90) noted that cautioning has three main objectives: to deal quickly and simply with less serious offenders, to divert them from the criminal courts (and thereby reduce the burden on the criminal justice system), and to reduce the chances of their re-offending. The Circular set out a framework of general principles and practices to provide national standards for cautioning. Chief Officers of Police were recommended, after discussion with the Crown Prosecution Service and other relevant agencies including the probation service and the local authority social service departments, to produce a force policy statement on cautioning which incorporated the new national standards, and to make arrangements to monitor the implementation of the policy.

7.4   The Circular noted that `a formal caution is a serious matter' because it is recorded by the police, it may influence them in their decision to institute proceedings if the person should offend again, and it may be cited in any subsequent court proceedings. The conditions which must be met before a caution may be administered are:

a. there must be evidence of the offender's guilt sufficient to give a realistic prospect of conviction, and

b. the offender must admit the offence, and

c. the offender (or in the case of a juvenile, his parents or guardian) must understand the significance of a caution and give informed consent to being cautioned.

7.5   When the first two conditions are met other factors which should be considered include the nature of the offence, the likely penalty if the offender were convicted by the court, their age and state of health, their previous criminal history, and their attitude to the offence including practical expressions of regret, and the views of the victim.

7.6   Cautioning seems a particularly appropriate way of dealing with minor drug offences and, as we have already noted, a very substantial proportion of drug offenders are cautioned, particularly where the offender is aged under 17 and when the offence is of unlawful possession of cannabis (see Chapter 2). However, in 1992 the cautioning rates of the 43 police forces in England and Wales for drug offences varied widely, ranging from 16 (West Yorkshire) to 77 (Kent) per cent.

7.7   The effectiveness of cautioning in reducing re-offending remains in question, although research suggests that for most first offenders the likelihood of reoffending is no greater than after conviction by the court[1].

---

[1]   Keith,S (1992) The criminal histories of those cautioned in 1985 and 1988. Home Office Research and Statistics Department, Research Bulletin No. 32, pp 44-46.

Research on Merseyside found that three quarters of those cautioned for a drug offence (98% for unlawful possession of cannabis) between 1987 and 1989 had not been dealt with for a further drug offence by the end of 1992, although some may have been convicted of other offences. First offenders were significantly less likely to be dealt with again for a drug offence during the follow-up period than those with previous cautions or convictions for any type of offence[2].

7.8   There is continuing criticism from sections of the public and the police that cautioning is a soft option. It is also suggested that some offenders might admit the offence and agree to a caution simply to have the matter dealt with speedily. Other concerns put to us included general ignorance about the procedure and, in particular, of the criteria used to make cautioning decisions.

7.9   It was against this background that in August 1991 we conducted our own survey of the 43 police forces in England and Wales seeking to understand their policies for cautioning drug offenders. We were very heartened by the fact that all but one force provided us with the information we sought.

SURVEY FINDINGS

Cautioning policy for drug offences

7.10   Twenty six (62 per cent) of the 42 police forces said they had a policy for cautioning persons arrested for drug offences, ten said they were presently reviewing their existing policies in the light of the 1990 Home Office Circular, and six said they had no specific policy. Whether or not forces had a policy for drug offences all said they would caution offenders possessing small quantities of cannabis for their own use, with 12 specifying `user' amounts ranging from one gram of resin or 3.5 grams of

---

2   Hughes,E and Hughes,S (1993) A Statistical Study of Cautioning of Drug Offenders on Merseyside in 1987, 1988 and 1989. University of Liverpool

herbal cannabis (four forces) to 14 grams of either. Only one of these forces quoted weights for other drugs. The other forces relied on the judgement of the arresting officer in estimating `user' amounts of drugs.

Offences and drugs considered for cautioning

7.11 Twenty six forces (62 per cent) said they would consider cautioning for offences other than unlawful possession with `minor social supply of cannabis with no profit', especially if it involved juveniles, being the most frequently cited example.

7.12 Eighteen forces said they would caution for an offence involving any drug in `user' amounts, four said they would depending on the merits of the case and whether the offender was helpful to the police in tracing a supplier, and two if the offender were receiving treatment for drug misuse. In all 24 forces (57 per cent) said that in some circumstances they would caution for any offence involving small quantities of any drug.

7.13 Nine forces said they would only caution for offences involving cannabis, one of which excluded cannabis oil. Two said they would caution if the offence involved any drug other than crack and six would caution only if the offence involved any, or specified, Class B or C drugs.

Effect of previous criminal history on decision to caution

7.14 Twenty two forces (52 per cent) said that a caution for a drug offence would not be precluded if the offender had previous cautions or convictions for any type of offence while nine would caution only if the offender had previously been dealt with for non-drugs offences. Eight forces would not caution if the offender had previously been dealt with for drugs offences, two would not caution if the offender had any previous cautions or convictions and the remaining two would consider each case on its merits.

Aggravating factors

7.15 The most frequently cited aggravating factors that would lead to a decision to put the case forward for prosecution by the Crown Prosecution Service to prosecute an offender who might otherwise be cautioned were: being charged with another offence committed at the same time, being suspected of supplying drugs or having previously or recently been dealt with for a drug offence.

7.16 Other factors cited which might be relevant to the decision to caution were helping the police to identify a drug supplier and if the offender was receiving treatment for drug misuse.

Second or subsequent cautions

7.17 Nine forces (21 per cent) said they would not give a caution for a second or subsequent drug offence. Fourteen (33 per cent) said they might depending on the merits of the case, and 19 (45 per cent) would consider further cautions in certain circumstances if, for example, there had been a long period since the first caution, the amount of drugs involved in the current offence was small, the offender assisted the police in further investigations, the offender was a juvenile, or was undergoing treatment for drug misuse.

Juveniles and adults

7.18 Rather more than a third of forces (38 per cent) said that different criteria were applied in making the decision to caution juveniles and adults but all considered that juveniles were more likely to be cautioned. Twelve forces noted that in the case of juvenile offenders there would be consultations with social services departments or other agencies if prosecution was being considered.

Authority of caution and time taken to make the decision

7.20 In almost two thirds (62 per cent) of the forces the decision to caution was made by an inspector whatever the drug or the offence, and in ten the force drug squad was consulted about the decision. A similar proportion of forces said that a caution would normally be administered between two and six weeks after the offender had been arrested; while 24 forces would administer 'instant' cautions shortly after arrest in 'straightforward' cases where the drug did not have to be analysed.

7.21 A quarter of the forces said they would give informal warnings for a drug offence depending on the merits and circumstances of the offence and usually only if juveniles were involved.

Referral to drug services

7.22 Only seven (17 per cent) of the forces did not operate, or plan to operate, some form of scheme for encouraging drug offenders to attend medical or drug services. This might consist of providing the offender with lists of the names, addresses and telephone numbers of the services as a matter of course or on request.

7.23 In no force did the decision to caution depend on the offender's expressed intention to attend a medical or drug service.

Retention and disclosure of records of cautioning

7.24 All forces retained records of cautions for at least three years while some retained them for five or twenty years or indefinitely.

7.25 Almost three quarters of the forces said they would disclose records of cautions to the court if the offender was subsequently prosecuted. Such records would also be disclosed to the local authority in child access cases or to other authorities in respect of applicants for specific occupations.

Supplementary survey

7.26 We later asked police forces to tell us whether their records of cautions included the age of the offender, gender, ethnic origin, any previous cautions or convictions and the type of drug involved in the offence. Thirty eight forces responded to the supplementary survey and 11 (29 per cent) recorded all the items listed while nine (24 per cent) recorded all but ethnic origin. All 38 forces recorded age, 35 gender, 29 previous cautions or convictions, 27 the drug involved in the offences and 18 the ethnic origin of the offender. When asked how this information was used, 21 forces (55 per cent) said for decisions on future disposals although in the main survey all had indicated that they took previous cautions or convictions into account in making the decision whether or not to caution. Only eight forces (21 per cent) said the information was used for management information purposes, including five who said it was used for monitoring their cautioning policy.

Conclusions

7.27 In 1991 all of the 42 police forces in England and Wales who provided responses to our survey said they would consider cautioning an offender for unlawful possession of cannabis in herbal or resin form and around sixty per cent said they would caution offenders for drug offences irrespective of the type of drug so long as small or `user' amounts were involved and whether or not the offender had been dealt with for drug or non-drug offences in the past. Forty per cent of forces said they would caution for minor supply offences, particularly if they involved juveniles, so long as they amounted to sharing small quantities of cannabis and with no profit to the supplier. Almost three quarters said they would caution more than once for drug offences depending on the merits and circumstances of the case. In straightforward cases according to force cautioning policy, and if the drug did not need to be analysed, 24 forces would administer an `instant' caution shortly after the offender was arrested.

7.28 A fifth of forces would not caution for offences other than unlawful possession of cannabis and ten restricted cautioning to first time offenders or to those being dealt with for a drug offence for the first time. There was plainly a reluctance on the part of many forces to caution adult offenders although most said they used the same criteria in making the decision to caution adults and juveniles.

7.29 Most forces operated some form of scheme to encourage drug offenders voluntarily to seek counselling, treatment or other form of support. None of the forces said that cautioning was conditional on the offender accepting such help.

7.30 Only eleven forces recorded all the information we thought was relevant to making further decisions to caution if the offender came to notice again for a drug offence. Eight forces said the information was used for management purposes, with five specifically referring to its use for monitoring their cautioning policy.

7.31 The responses to our survey showed that, while remaining consistent with the spirit and guidance contained in the 1990 Home Office circular, there were wide variations in the policies adopted and operated by individual forces. This has resulted in considerable variations in cautioning rates between them which cannot be explained merely as responses to differing circumstances across the country.

7.32 A number of arguments have been put to us, by the police and by others, in favour of national guidelines for cautioning drug offenders. There may be others, perhaps some senior police officers, who will see such specific guidance as a threat to the discretion of the police. Such guidance could not, of course, be prescriptive as operational discretion remains, as ever, with individual Chief Officers. However, we see many advantages for the police and the public, in a national policy for cautioning drug offenders with the appearance as well as the reality of fairness, which is well understood and consistently administered and effectively monitored. **We endorse recommendation 109 of the Royal Commission on Criminal Justice, which stated that cautioning should be governed by statute, under which national guidelines should be laid down in regulations.**

7.33 **We recommend that national guidelines for the cautioning of drug offences should be drawn up which are in**

addition to the general principles contained in the 1990
Home Office circular. The guidelines should cover the
following:

* the nature of the offence

* the quantity of drug involved

* the characteristics of the offender, including age and
  history of previous drugs and non-drugs offences

* the method of administering the caution, including
  the rank of the officer making the decision, the time
  between the arrest and the caution

* ensuring the offender understands the nature of the
  caution, perhaps by a written statement

* encouraging offenders to make contact with medical
  and drug services where appropriate

7.34 We do not suggest that the guidelines should be specific on the
questions of offences, types of drug or quantities of drug. Only cautioning
offences which involve Class B drugs could, for example, imply that the
misuse of these drugs is viewed less seriously. In our view, cautioning
would be a viable option for dealing with a drug offence when all the
circumstances of the case and of the offender satisfy the general criteria for
cautioning as well as those suggested by the guidelines. We have not heard
any evidence to suggest that any particular method of administering a
caution, or that the interval between the offence and the caution, increased
the effectiveness of cautioning in reducing further offending. But in devising
the guidelines we would suggest that the effect of these factors on the
impact of a caution should be considered. In this context, we note

recommendation 111 of the Royal Commission on Criminal Justice. This recommends an examination of the possibility of combining the caution with a requirement on the offender to co-operate with social work agencies or the probation service or to agree to consult a doctor or attend a clinic, perhaps under the overall responsibility of the probation service. We see difficulties in applying such a requirement to drug offenders. In any case it is already common practice for the police to offer to put drug misusers in contact with advice and treatment services and we support this approach.

7.35   It seems an appropriate time to consider extending the cautioning of drug offenders in the way in which we have suggested. The results of our survey were made available to the police and we were encouraged by the decision of the Association of Chief Officers of Police to conduct their own review of force cautioning policies which as we report is still in progress.

7.36   Shortly after our inquiry, the 1990 Home Office Circular was replaced by Home Office Circular 18/1994. This circular discourages the use of cautioning for the most serious of offences especially those triable only on indictment; it also encourages greater consistency between forces and more accurate recording of cautions. Our recommendations fall well within these criteria.

8. Other Alternatives to Prosecution

8.1   In addition to our detailed consideration of the use of cautioning by the police, we also looked at two other alternatives to prosecution which have application to cases involving drugs. These are the compounding procedures used by HM Customs and Excise and the power to discontinue prosecutions which may be exercised by the Crown Prosecution Service. We suspect there is a general lack of awareness as to how these processes operate and, in our view more should be done to publicise their existence and monitor their fair and effective operation.

Compounding

8.2   Under the Customs and Excise Management Act 1979 it is an offence to be knowingly concerned with the evasion or attempted evasion of any prohibition or restriction in force which includes the import of controlled drugs.   Such offenders may be prosecuted and, if convicted sentenced accordingly by a court of law.   The same legislation also empowers Customs and Excise to compound proceedings which means, in essence, that the offender is allowed to pay a fixed penalty in lieu of prosecution. We were told that compounding is a procedure widely used by Customs, not just in drug cases.   In the five years from 1987 - 1992 compounding involving drugs was used in 522, 733, 1063, 1184, 1066 and 718 cases . The criteria adopted, which are agreed with Home Office, limit the use of compounding to offences involving herbal cannabis or resin not exceeding total weight of 10 grammes. Offenders who meet the criteria are given the option to "compound" for a penalty on a sliding scale from £50 - £75. Should the offender commit another similar offence within five years prosecution is automatic.

8.3   Although, unlike court proceedings, details of compounded proceedings are not generally made public, offenders who accept a compounded settlement are advised that details may be disclosed to third parties in any of the following circumstances:

- To the Court, if there is a prosecution for a similar offence within five years;

To an employer if:

- the nature of the offender's job helped him to commit the offence, or

- the offender's job requires a particularly high degree of unimpaired faculties or judgement;

- To other Government Departments whose responsibilities are affected by the offence;

- To Parliament if the case attracts public attention and disclosure would be in the public interest.

The stated purpose of compounding is that it avoids prolonged and costly court proceedings for both sides. Customs refute, however, that it should be regarded either as an out of court settlement or an on the spot fine. Unfortunately we were unable to obtain any information about the rate at which offenders who accept a compounded offer are subsequently convicted of another drugs offence. We recognise the value of compounding in keeping a number of relatively minor offenders out of the courts. **As with cautioning, we recommend that compounding be extended to drugs other than cannabis.**

Discontinuance and the Crown Prosecution Service (CPS)

8.4 Discontinuance is a specific power given to the CPS under the Prosecution of Offences Act 1985. It is an important but not the only method by which a Crown Prosecutor can bring a case to an end. Case files submitted by the police to the CPS are reviewed in the context of criteria set out in the Code for Crown Prosecutors which is published under the provisions of the Act. The review process is regarded as one of the most important tasks of the CPS because it gives practical effect to the theory of the independence of the Service. The CPS exercises an independent judgement about the case presented to it and decides on the basis of the tests laid down in the Code whether or not to advise the police to institute proceedings or allow proceedings already commenced to proceed to court.

8.5   The first test which must be met if a case is to be proceeded with is that of evidential sufficiency. There must be admissible, substantial and reliable evidence that a criminal offence has been committed sufficient to support a realistic prospect of conviction. If a case meets this test, the prosecutor must go on to consider whether the public interest requires a prosecution and this is the area which has been of particular interest to us. The Code contains a non-exhaustive list of factors for the Crown Prosecutor to consider in reaching a decision. Every case involves weighing different factors which arise from the offence, the offender or the victim. In a case where there is sufficient evidence to proceed, the discretion vested in a Crown Prosecutor not to proceed on public interest grounds is an important safeguard to the defendant and its existence seeks to ensure that the administration of criminal law operates with a measure of compassion.

8.6   We heard that the prosecutor can receive information from a number of sources to assist in determining the balance of the public interest. For example; it may be supplied by the police on file, from the probation service, social services departments of local authorities or from the defendant's doctor through his legal representative.

8.7   If at any time a Crown Prosecutor decides that the case should proceed no further, he or she will terminate the proceedings. Depending on the stage which the proceedings have reached, this can be effected by applying to the Magistrates' Court for leave to withdraw the proceedings, by offering no evidence or by giving written notice of discontinuance to the clerk of the Magistrates' Court. No evidence can also be offered in the

Crown Court although the CPS does not have discontinuance powers in the Crown Court. In this context, the Code particularly mentions the need to have regard to the Home Office cautioning guidelines. Proceedings instituted in circumstances which appear to fall outside the spirit of the guidelines are queried with the police and may be discontinued where the Crown Prosecutor is satisfied that the proceedings would not be in the public interest. We were given as an example an offence involving possession of a small amount of cannabis for personal use, where the police would normally caution but for some reason had not done so. The prosecutor would make enquiries of the police and if satisfied the caution would have been appropriate, would discontinue the case. In this context, **we endorse recommendation 110 of the Royal Commission on Criminal Justice, under which the CPS would be able to require the police to administer a caution in lieu of prosecution, provided that the defendant admitted the offence.** Discontinuance is, however, circumscribed by the stage which proceedings have reached. Cases may not be discontinued after the accused has been committed for trial or after the magistrates have begun to hear evidence in a summary or either way trial. This means that a case must then be terminated by the prosecutor offering no evidence, if he or she takes the view that it is no longer proper to continue with it on either evidential or public interest grounds.

Assessment

8.8   Assessment of discontinuance has been carried out through the Public Interest Case Assessment (PICA) experiment. This had its origins in a paper produced in 1986 by the Association of Chief Officers of Probation (ACOP) which examined how the probation service might work with the newly-formed CPS on a number of pre-trial issues. The paper identified the possible lack of personal information concerning the defendant on the police file and introduced the idea of PICA schemes by which it was proposed that the probation service should provide the CPS with:

".... sound, verified and relevant information describing a defendant's personal circumstances which could assist the Crown Prosecutors to reach an informed decision as to the merits of discontinuing a case on public interest grounds".

The Vera Institute of Justice in conjunction with the CPS and the probation service designed and evaluated an experimental PICA at an Inner London Court. This joint initiative was well received and attracted interest from other criminal justice agencies. This led in turn to pilot schemes being set up in 1991 in Greater Manchester, Northumbria and West Midlands. These schemes are in the process of being evaluated by the Home Office Research and Planning Unit with particular reference to their costs and benefits.

8.9   Our inquiries into discontinuance were hampered by a lack of offence specific data on rates for drug cases. Discontinuance figures do not, in any event, distinguish between evidential and public interest grounds. We would have liked to make comparisons between cautioning rates and those for discontinuance in the same area. Home Office statistics for drug offences cases showed that in 1992 in England and Wales 977 drug cases had been discontinued compared to 358 in 1990. Almost half of the discontinued cases were in London.

8.10 It was clear that whether representations about discontinuance were made probably depended on the level of awareness of this particular aspect of CPS practice. We gathered that it is not usual for drug agencies to be involved in putting forward a case for discontinuance on behalf of an unrepresented defendant. Although more representations would have resource implications, we have been assured that the CPS would not seek to limit an increase in representations on that ground and that all representations made on a defendant's behalf would be carefully considered. In cases where legal representation was not available there were concerns that defendants might not be able to make adequate representations to the CPS for discontinuance or be aware that such a possibility existed. It was not clear to us how the CPS developed policy in the area of public interest and whether public opinion was an influence. We were told, however, that efforts were continuingly being made by the CPS to standardise policy across the country to achieve a greater consistency.

8.11 Clearly, discontinuance has the potential for contributing both to the cost effectiveness of the criminal justice system and, in the case of drug misusers, to reducing the harm to individuals and the community. The CPS are in a unique position to assess the whole case, both from the evidential and public interest stand point. They are in a position to assess information, particularly on a defendant's personal and medical background, which would not come the way of the police or any other single agency. Discontinuance should also provide a useful backstop for the cautioning process. The effectiveness of this depends on good communications between the CPS and the police, operating agreed guidelines which we have proposed should be drawn up on a national basis for drug cases.

8.12 Discontinuance also has a harm reduction aspect. An example we considered was the benefits to society and the individual of not interrupting a defendant's drug treatment programme by legal proceedings ending in a court case. So long as discontinuance and the criteria for it remain little known, however, there will be too many cases where relevant information about a defendant will not be put forward for assessment. It is apparent that the process is not well understood, particularly by agencies who may have something to contribute. The Royal Commission on Criminal Justice has recommended that subject to the planned evaluation of existing PICA schemes, these should be put on a formal and systematic basis and extended as far as practicable across the country. Whilst welcoming this proposal, we note that the PICA pilot schemes excluded offences under the Misuse of Drugs Act and that the Probation Service is not the only potential source of verified information. The PICA pilot scheme model is unlikely to represent the precise shape of future co-operation, but with more widespread understanding of how discontinuance works, probation and other agencies will be better placed to advise on decisions which the CPS must take. In the context of drugs misuse, the objective of enhancing community safety will mean that the public interest is not always best served by the intervention of the formal criminal justice system when other interventions targeted specifically at the drugs problem are available. **We recommend that the CPS and drug agencies adopt a pro-active approach to publicising the criteria for discontinuance on public interest grounds.**

9. Health Care Issues for Drug Misusers in Police Custody

9.1   The medical care of drug misusers in police custody is a problematic area. As in the case of mentally disordered offenders, there are the difficult questions of identification, fitness for detention and fitness for interview. Beyond those, there are issues about the treatment of those using drugs on arrest. We have considered these questions and taken evidence from several sources, including police surgeons. From the evidence we received, we were struck by the differences between policy and approach to treatment, and by the uncertainties with regard to the statutory requirements of the Misuse of Drugs Act.

9.2   In a report prepared for the Royal Commission on Criminal Justice it was estimated that between 1,500 - 2,000 doctors are employed as police surgeons in the UK. The same report records that in 11% of a sample of cases dealt with by police surgeons the main reason for the doctor being called was that the detainee was suffering from the effects of drugs (with or without alcohol). A number of these detainees were notified addicts and some had been prescribed Methadone. For reasons we outline later in this chapter we believe that drug misusers make up a much greater proportion of those detained in police custody than are identified as requiring immediate medical attention.

9.3   A number of concerns were put to us regarding the medical treatment of drug misusers in police custody. We heard that a major concern for drug misusers themselves was whether they would have access to medical help. The quality of treatment provided by police surgeons was said to vary considerably. While some were happy to work within drug treatment regimes already established by consultants others chose to disregard existing programmes. Treatment policies were said to vary widely across the country. In some areas, misusers continued to receive prescribed medication. Where good liaison with local treatment clinics existed clinic workers were able to take medication to police stations for their clients. In other areas, including the Metropolitan Police, we were told that it was unusual for misusers to be enabled to continue a regime of prescribed methadone. We recognise that decisions on medical treatment are very much a matter for individual clinical judgement but we question whether blanket policies, such as preventing misusers from continuing to take prescribed methadone, can be justified as being in the best interests of the detainee.

Guidelines on Fitness for Interview

9.4   Police surgeons are called on from time to time to establish whether a detainee, who is apparently under the influence of drugs, withdrawing or known or suspected of being a misuser, is fit to be interviewed by a police officer and, in extreme cases, fit to be detained in a police station. We were told that certifying fitness for interviewing such cases had assumed greater importance in recent years due in part to the provision of PACE, an increase in the number of drug misusers and an increasing tendency for fitness at time of interview to feature as an issue in court. The PACE Codes of Practice offer little on fitness for interview in these circumstances except to note that, with certain exceptions, "No person who is unfit through drink or drugs to the extent that he is unable to appreciate the significance of question put to him and his answers may be questioned about an alleged offence in that condition.............". We see merit in devising guidelines for establishing fitness for interview and fitness to be detained to assist police surgeons.

Guidelines on the medical care of detainees

9.5   Guidance on the medical care of detainees is contained in the Codes of Practice for the Police and Criminal Evidence Act 1984 (PACE) and in guidelines on clinical management produced by a Department of Health working group on drug misuse and dependence. The PACE Codes of Practice contains the following guidance:

"If a detained person requests a medical examination the police surgeon must be called as soon as practicable. He may in addition be examined by a medical practitioner of his own choice at his own expense."

The Codes also stipulate that if a detainee is required to take any medication in compliance with medical directions then the custody officer is responsible for its safekeeping and for ensuring that he is given the opportunity to take the medication at the appropriate time. No police officer may administer controlled drugs subject to the Misuse of Drugs Act 1971 for this purpose and a detainee may administer such drugs to himself only under the personal supervision of the police surgeon.

The advice contained in the "Guidelines on Clinical Management" include the following:

"A drug misuser who has been detained should be seen as soon as possible by a doctor for assessment. Medical assessment should include whether the patient is fit to be detained or interviewed.

Prompt treatment to limit or prevent withdrawal symptoms will help to reduce the risk of disturbed behaviour in custody and ensure that the patient is fit to be interviewed.

A police surgeon is usually prepared to provide a short term prescription to allow a sick person in custody to continue the medical treatment which he has been receiving. The same consideration should apply to drug misusers who are receiving a prescription of Methadone or another drug as a treatment for drug misuse."

9.6   We were told of several difficulties arising from guidance advocating the continuing administration of prescribed drugs. First there was the problem of cost involved in a doctor returning to a police station periodically to administer medication to a detainee, thereby resulting in a fee on each occasion for an individual consultation rather than a sessional charge. There were also said to be problems in storing controlled drugs at police stations although there are no regulatory requirements on storage to prevent this happening. It was also suggested that if it became common knowledge that drugs such as Methadone were available at police stations some misusers would be desperate enough to seek arrest in order to see a doctor and gain access to controlled drugs. **Despite the apparent difficulties, we recommend that the treatment options for drug misusers in custody be examined and that jointly-agreed guidelines be developed.** We wish to encourage, therefore, the development of the contacts we understand have already taken place between representatives of police surgeons and the relevant professional bodies to consider these treatment issues. We understand that a joint working group has been established involving representatives of the Association of Police Surgeons, Royal College of Psychiatrists and other relevant professional bodies. The working group will report in due course on the management of individuals in police custody with substance misuse problems and dependence. More contact and exchange visits involving drug treatment specialists would also help to develop better understanding of the work of these two professional groups.

9.7 **From the evidence we have heard, we recognise the difficulties of treating drug misusers in custody. We recommend, however, that good practice requires that:**

    1) **If a detainee is already being treated for drug dependence with substitute medication, such as methadone, this should be continued whilst he/she is in custody. Efforts should be made to confirm the current prescription by contacting the doctor and/or clinic concerned, or the retail pharmacist who dispenses the prescription. If the detainee's own medication cannot be obtained, the police surgeon should issue a private prescription.**

2) If a detainee is not under current treatment (or details of any such treatment cannot be verified) but nevertheless has a clear history and signs of regular drug use and objective evidence of withdrawal symptoms, treatment should be given to alleviate the severity of withdrawal symptoms.

We recommend that the guidelines in preparation on medical care incorporate these procedures.

9.8   We considered the employment of specialist nursing staff in the health care of drug misusing detainees which we heard is the practice in some parts of Australia. In February 1992 a tiered health care system for persons in police custody within the Melbourne Metropolitan area was implemented. This utilises a forensic nurse for the primary contact, with forensic medical officers providing medical consultation and support as necessary. Public hospital emergency departments and a secure hospital ward constituted the third tier for medical problems needing hospitalisation. Criteria were developed setting out the delineation between the forensic nurse and the forensic medical officer. The nurses, all psychiatrically trained, were recruited from within the corrections health system and were provided with transport, communication and basic medical supplies. This enables a flexible response to be made to requests for medical attention and for the nurse to make a basic medical assessment and administer appropriate treatment. Under medical guidance the nurses are able to supply and dispense medication including methadone, perform wound care, assess the need for transport to hospital and to liaise with the prison system to establish priorities for prisoner transfer. This system has now been running for over twelve months and, we understand, the results so far have been promising.

9.9   Despite the differences between the systems pertaining to Australia and the UK, we believe similar arrangements could be introduced which would enhance the care available to drug misusers in custody as well as reduce the costs of providing it. Although the UK does not currently have a qualified prison nursing service, there are other sources which would provide recruits to such schemes including trained mental health nurses (CPN's) currently working in diversion schemes, those employed in community drug teams, and those Nurse Practitioners who are already being employed in a range of outreach facilities. We are of the opinion that the increased use of such nurses in liaison with police surgeons would enable a more comprehensive service to be delivered. **We recommend piloting the employment of specialist nursing staff in police stations.**

Identification and notification of drug misusing detainees

9.10   We have already suggested earlier in this chapter that a significantly greater proportion of misusers are examined by police surgeons then are recorded as suffering from the effects of drugs.   In our Part I report on community resources and the probation service we noted that attempts to identify individual misusers are often thwarted by their reluctance to disclose past or present misuse of illegal drugs to anyone associated with the Criminal Justice System.   A number of obstacles to self disclosure were identified.   Those of particular relevance to our current study include the prospect that disclosure of drug misuse might adversely affect a decision about bail, given the perceived lack of suitable bail hostel accommodation willing to accept drug misusers.   Lack of guarantees for the confidentiality of personal information was also thought to be a significant disincentive. Drug misusers are unclear about whether information on their drug misuse would be shared between treatment, probation and social services, the police and prisons, and no doubt many assume the worst.   Given that these and other disincentives were seen as formidable barriers to disclosure in the context of the probation service, it is even more likely that individuals in police custody will be reluctant to disclose misuse.

9.11   We consider, however, that police surgeons have an important part to play in encouraging self disclosure.   There will be many occasions when a misuser's contact with criminal justice agencies following arrest will be limited to the police and probably a police surgeon. Clearly this will be the case when a detainee is released with a caution or without being charged. Nevertheless, there is still in our view an opportunity which should not be missed to address a misuser's drug problem. We have already endorsed the adoption of harm reduction principles by the police and their role in a multi-agency approach to tackling drug misuse. In our view, there is also an opportunity for police surgeons to play a part in attempting to put misusers in touch with treatment and rehabilitation agencies. This pre-supposes that misusers can be identified and contacts developed and sustained between police surgeons and drugs services. **We recommend that police surgeons should ask all detainees about the possibility of drug misuse and take this opportunity to put misusers in contact with treatment and rehabilitation agencies.**

9.12 A further reason for police surgeons to take all reasonable steps to identify drug misusers in custody is to satisfy the notification requirements of the Misuse of Drug (Notification of and Supply to Addicts) Regulations 1973. Section 3 of the regulations requires "any doctor who attends a person who he considers or has reasonable grounds to suspect, is addicted to a controlled drug mentioned in the schedule to the regulations" (which include cocaine and heroin) to notify the Home Office Addicts Index. The Addicts Index helps to maintain controls on the prescribing of controlled drugs in three ways:

- by allowing doctors to check the current status of an addict who is seeking treatment;

- by identifying the emergence of a new or different prescribing source;

- by providing information to assist the Drugs Inspectorate in its investigation when police inspection of a chemist's register has highlighted an unusual or irregular supply of controlled drugs.

An ACMD Working Group set up to examine the usefulness of the Index recommended in 1990 that it remained essential to the monitoring of prescribing practice and as a reference to doctors who are treating addict patients. The working group further recommended that the Index should be kept in place.

9.13 It was clear from evidence put to us that there is considerable uncertainty amongst police surgeons as to the requirements of the notification regulations. This is also borne out by the comparatively low level of notifications from this source. A common misapprehension amongst police surgeons appears to be that there is no need to notify an individual already in treatment, although this is not the case. We heard that a small survey of the records of people arrested and charged with offences, conducted in one city during spring 1992, identified 10 people who were described as notifiable drug users. A check of the Addicts Index showed that 6 of the 10 had not been notified as addicts by September 1993. Of the four who had been notified at some time before their current arrest, or shortly afterwards, none were notified by the police surgeon. These included one man who had been prescribed methadone from a local Drug Dependence Unit on the day of his arrest. **We recommend that the Home Office considers ways of clarifying for police surgeons the notification requirements of the relevant Regulations, perhaps in conjunction with the Association of Police Surgeons, and that the guidance being prepared should include reference to this matter.**

Confidentiality

9.14 Clearly the examination of detainees and identification and notification of misusers raises difficult questions of medical confidentiality, or at least in convincing a detainee the principles of confidentiality will be maintained. A complicating factor here is the "forensic" aspects of a police surgeon's role in, for example, examining suspects or victims and taking samples which may form part of the evidence in a court case. We heard that brief medical notes were recorded and retained at police stations but more detailed confidential notes were kept by the police surgeon and did not travel with the prisoner.

Training

9.15 We recognise the difficulties surrounding much of the work of police surgeons. Often detainees are unwilling or unable to co-operate, no medical records are available on many of the individuals concerned and examinations take place in less than ideal surroundings and often during unsocial hours. We do not question that the vast majority of police surgeons have the well being of detainees, as for any other patient, as their main concern. The wide variation in treatment responses, however, suggests to us that more training is needed in dealing with drug misuse. We were told that most police surgeons were GPs who received little or no training in drug misuse after completing their final examinations. A training course for new entrant police surgeons has been established and we understand that the Association of Police Surgeons are keen to extend training for doctors already working in this field. As always, the provision of training raises resource issues and we were warned that, if it becomes a requirement, it may act as a disincentive to some doctors who may consider becoming police surgeons. **We recommend that the professional bodies concerned give consideration to the specific training needs of police surgeons in treating drug misusers.**

AIDS and drug misusers in custody

9.16 The advent of AIDS posed a particular challenge to the police, as it did to prison officers and health care workers, in appearing to expose them to special risks in the course of their work. This led to considerable anxiety in police forces and their response had three main elements:

- the introduction of operational precautions, including protective clothing and suitable cleaning procedures for situations where officers were exposed to body fluids;

- recording HIV information (from whatever source) on the Police National Computer by way of the contagious warning marker;

- recording of HIV status on the Exceptional Risks form which accompanies the transfer of prisoners considered to pose a special risk, particularly movements between police forces and prisons.

9.17 Home Office Circular 72/1988 was the first guidance to police on AIDS and while it stressed the low risk to police officers in the course of their duties, it dealt entirely with operational safety measures and not with other responses concerned with the identification of HIV infected prisoners. No reference was made to the fact that the majority of HIV infected people in custody were unlikely to know their HIV status; nor was it mentioned there was a greater risk to all staff from their own private behaviour. Finally, the Circular did not comment on the advantages of education and training in this area.

9.18 Over the years, anxiety seems to have decreased and with it the incidence of exaggerated responses, particularly wearing unnecessary protective clothing. Information of HIV status continues, however, to be recorded nationally and locally. These practices have come under increasing criticism on the following grounds:

- identifying HIV status can increase the risks in so far as it encourages precautions only where a person is known or rumoured to be HIV positive;

- traffic in confidential information can discourage the self identification of those infected or at risk, particularly in respect of substantial numbers of drug misusers, and it can also act as a barrier to co-operation with other agencies who adopt strict confidentiality.

The criticisms have been fuelled by reported incidents of HIV information being passed on or coming to the notice of those outside the criminal justice system, including via the practice in some police stations of displaying HIV status on cells or records.

9.19   There has been a growing view that the police should abandon these practices in their own interests and adopt the same rigorous safety precautions towards all detainees, whether or not their HIV status is known, as is the practice in the health care sector. The ACMD in its AIDS and Drug Misuse Report (1989) also took the view that it was not necessary for anyone beyond medical and nursing staff to know about the HIV status of anyone in custody. These views have been given added impetus by the notable progress that has been made within the Prison Service towards attaining the same objectives, including the abandonment of VIR. Early in our enquiries, we were told that some prisons no longer accept or record information on HIV status from the Exceptional Risks form, nor pass on such information to the police except through medical channels.

9.20   The group has heard evidence from police forces who recognise the limited usefulness of the PNC marker and of recorded HIV status but have nevertheless told the Group that they would not wish to continue this practice in the light of the continued concerns of police officers and their families. In view of this evidence of a current disparity in practice and attitude, we commend the new circular, "HIV/AIDS : Guidance to the Police Service" (113/92) which has now been issued and to which we were given access during our enquiries by the Home Office Working Group concerned. It represents major progress in this area and we believe provides a framework for police practice to develop in the best interests of the force and in line with that of other relevant agencies, including the Prison and

Health Services. The purpose of this circular is to promote :

- Safe practices and procedures in relation to operational situations which may pose a risk of infection from HIV and other blood borne infections such as Hepatitis B.

- A greater awareness amongst police officers and civilians about HIV/AIDS thus reducing unnecessary fear.

- The sensitive and informed treatment of people who have HIV infection.

- To recommend, following the institution of adequate training and safe working practices that the practice of recording HIV information about persons with police records, other than on confidential medical records, is ended.

9.21 We recognise that the implementation of this guidance will require determination and commitment from chief officers. Translating policy into accepted practice will depend upon effective education and training at all levels including probationers. Until now this appears to have been sparse and patchy. We endorse the importance attached to training and welcome, therefore, the awareness training course for police officers which the Home Office is in the process of developing. This is designed to promote safe practice and procedures in operational situations by the practice of universal precautions and to promote a sensitive and informed professional approach to the issues surrounding HIV/AIDS and Hepatitis B. We welcome this advance, particularly as the problem of Hepatitis B has not always received adequate coverage in the past. **We therefore recommend that the HIV/AIDS and Hepatitis B training course being developed for police officers is implemented as a matter of urgency and that progress in this area is monitored by HM Inspectorate of Constabulary.**

9.22 We have been interested in current examples of good practice. A joint working initiative set up by a police force with its local needle exchange scheme increased officers' knowledge and understanding of HIV/AIDS and reduced their fears. We recommend this as one of several possible approaches within a multi-agency context and **recommend that chief officers explore the possibilities of joint training with local HIV and drugs agencies for their staff.**

10. Performance Measurement and Ethnic Monitoring

10.1 Our report outlines a new approach to the policing of drug misuse based on the idea of a set of objectives which should come to be shared by police, treatment and educational agencies. We have noted that historically it has proved difficult to manage the implementation of new policing policies on the ground. Many innovations have been devised but the discretion and operational autonomy of constables has worked against innovation in practice.

10.2 Recently, a direct attack on this problem has been mounted by the introduction of "Police Service performance indicators" for the police. This system of monitoring what the police do was placed on a statutory basis by the Local Government Act 1992. However, the performance indicators which are envisaged are relatively simple measures such as the average time taken to respond to a 999 call. More sophisticated qualitative monitoring is carried out by HM Inspectorate of Constabulary in both regional and thematic inspections. During inspections, HMIs have the opportunity to ask detailed questions and probe for valid and reliable responses from chief officers.

10.3 From the evidence we have heard, we do not consider that a stage has been reached in the development of local and street level strategies where appropriate quantitative performance indicators can be defined. Indeed, we think premature selection of indicators in this field might seriously distort the way in which this sensitive area of policing is carried out. However, we do believe that it is possible to frame appropriate questions for HMIs to ask on a regular basis during inspections. The answers to the questions we have in mind would indicate progress towards the implementation of the approach we have outlined in this report.

10.4 Undoubtedly, once it becomes known that such questions are going to be asked, Chief Officers will set about the task of obtaining the necessary information from local commanders and the agencies with which they work. This process, which should involve close consultation with those responsible for a wide variety of communities with a corresponding variety of drug problems, may well lead to the development of performance measures which would be both meaningful and useful. This "bottom up" approach to the development of indicators is more likely to gain acceptance and commitment in this working environment in which, we have argued, multi-agency collaboration is both essential and difficult to achieve.

10.5 **The three main areas of activity which we have recommended the police and other relevant agencies should develop are:**

- **consultation and the adoption of a common purpose**

- **development of local, integrated strategies**

- **application of the principles of harm reduction in the implementation of these strategies**

In order to monitor police progress in each of these areas we recommend that the HMIC considers posing the following questions as part of the routine inspection process:

- **What structure(s) exist within the Force for consultation with other agencies concerning drug misuse?**

- **Whether a strategy has been devised with other agencies to limit both the demand and supply of drugs?**

- **And, finally, how enforcement strategies take account of harm reduction and community damage limitation principles.**

10.6 A further impetus towards achieving the declared goals of effective multi-agency co-operation and the adoption of harm reduction principles in policing individuals and the community could come from the Home Office White Paper on police reform published in June 1993. The recommendations include requirements to consult local people and the development of strategies for involving them in the preparation of local policing plans. The White Paper actively encourages partnership and requires objectives to be declared for achieving community involvement. The HMI's questions and inspection process, taken together with declared objectives on partnership, should enable the police planning and performance in this area to be monitored effectively.

Ethnic Monitoring

10.7 Drug misuse is an area where ethnic monitoring is especially important as enforcement activities can appear to bear particularly on these groups. The concerns of ethnic minority communities regarding the way they are affected by drugs policing activities such as stop and search, and for that matter by the criminal justice system in general, reinforces the importance of effective ethnic monitoring. An important development towards enabling the police service and other agencies in the criminal justice system to ensure that they deliver a fair and non-discriminatory service to all members of the public and to employees is to be found in Section 95 of the Criminal Justice Act 1991. This provides that:

> "the Secretary of State shall in each year publish such information as he considers expedient for the purposes of .... facilitating the performance of persons (engaged in the administration of criminal justice) of their duty to avoid discrimination against any persons on the grounds of race or sex or any other improper ground."

The requirements of the Act extend to the police service and the first report, "Race and the Criminal Justice System 1992" was published in September 1992. This was largely based on information already collected but it is envisaged that more comprehensive information will be required in the future to fulfil the provisions of the Act. A Home Office circular, issued in July 1992, to police on Section 95 urged the early adoption of standard ethnic classification systems, including the 9 point self classification and 4 point third party classification system. **We endorse recommendations 2 and 3 of the Royal Commission on Criminal Justice which called for further research into the extent of discrimination against ethnic minorities in the criminal justice system and the introduction of a system of ethnic monitoring to establish how ethnic minorities are treated and identify the measures to ensure that the criminal justice system is applied in the same way to all.**

10.8 We welcome these developments as monitoring systems available until now have clearly been inadequate. The police stop/search record which has been used includes a race code section but we were told that this was used with only varying reliability and the race information contained in the forms was not collected centrally. Moreover, our survey into cautions indicated that only a minority of police forces undertook ethnic monitoring of cautioning practices. We understand that a working group on police statistics has been considering the inclusion of an ethnic marker on police forms and that the Police Inspectorate are developing ethnic indicators for their quality of service assessments which include stop and search activities. We were also interested to learn that at least one force monitors complaints by ethnic grouping.

10.9 We attach great importance to the ethnic monitoring of police activities in the field of drug misuse. We have already pointed to the coincedence between areas of high drug misuse in our inner cities and concentration of ethnic minority communities in these areas. This means inevitably that such communities will be particularly exposed to vigorous street level enforcement against drug misuse. It is, therefore, essential that police activities not only are non-discriminatory but can be shown to be so. Open and consistent ethnic monitoring will help to establish confidence within communities, promote partnerships and cooperation between agencies, and increase police credibility. **We recommend that senior police managers clearly demonstrate the importance which they attach to ethnic monitoring returns and the performance of their forces in this respect, and ensure that the necessary training to achieve this is in place.**

11. Summary of Recommendations

Current Enforcement Strategies

1.   We recommend that a range of approaches, tailored to local circumstances and enforcement objectives, should be developed. We support the identification by the police of a set of street level strategies with likely outcomes on which local communities can be consulted and informed. This would enable the police to intervene more quickly in drug related incidents and in a more considered way. (3.4)

2.   We regard stop and search as an essential element of the street level policing providing there is quality control and that outcomes are properly monitored. (3.10)

3.   There is a need for local initiatives to take account of local differences and for the police to get over to communities the various options available to the police and the reasons for adopting particular strategies. (3.12)

A Harm Reduction Approach

4.   We recommend the wider adoption of harm reduction principles in developing enforcement strategies. (4.2)

5.   We recommend that an enforcement strategy which aims to limit the harm to individuals and damage to the community from drug misuse should have the following characteristics:

> [i]   Where choices have to be made between enforcement operations against different kinds of drugs, the drug which causes most harm should be the principal target. It will not always be possible for policing strategies to target individual drugs given the extent of polydrug misuse, but the enforcement process can take this into account.

[ii] If possible, where choices have to be made between enforcement operations, priority should be given to early intervention to eliminate drug dealing sites, particularly new locations, before these have the chance to establish and advertise themselves.

[iii] Enforcement should support the efforts of other agencies working to reduce the harm caused by drug misuse.

[iv] A recognition that harm reduction has a part to play in returning areas to normality through improvements to the environment, such as better street lighting, public buildings and amenities. (4.4)

6.   We recommend that a range of criteria should be adopted to judge the effectiveness of applying harm reduction principles to street level drug enforcement. (4.5)

Multi-Agency Working

7.   In promoting effective joint action to tackle the problems associated with drug misuse, we recommend:

- The establishment of a common purpose between all the agencies involved.

- Recognition of the essential role of local authorities

- The development of effective structures under which agencies can co-operate and on which they are represented, in order to identify strategic objectives, and monitor progress.

- Investment in the partnership through the designation of responsible staff and the provision of adequate time for them to develop it.

- The development within these partnership arrangements of local alliances to plan and implement specific programmes of action.

- Engaging the local media in the efforts being made.

- Adequate resourcing of these activities by the authorities which commission and purchase services and, in particular, the recognition by those authorities that the promotion of community safety is a legitimate and necessary element of the response to drug misuse.

- The sharing of information by all the partners.

- Regular monitoring and reporting on progress in establishing partnerships and alliances by the inspecting arms of the relevant agencies, including police, health and social services inspectorates. (5.19)

Policing Youth Culture

8.   We recommend that the organisation of more legal raves be encouraged by local authorities exercising maximum discretion in the granting of licences and by involving responsible organisers of raves in the process. (6.10)

9.   We recommend that the criteria for the granting of licences for raves and other such events by local authorities should include:

- availability of free cold water

- provision of rest facilities in a cool environment

- monitoring of temperature and air quality

- provision of information and advice on drugs.

- compliance with a regulatory scheme for the selection, training and management of door staff (6.10)

Cautioning

10. We endorse recommendation 109 of the Royal Commission on Criminal Justice, which stated that cautioning should be governed by statute, under which national guidelines should be laid down in regulations. (7.32)

11. We recommend that national guidelines for the cautioning of drug offences should be drawn up which are in addition to the general principles contained in the 1990 Home Office circular. The guidelines should cover the following:

* the nature of the offence

* the quantity of drug involved

* the characteristics of the offender, including age and history of previous drugs and non-drugs offences

* the method of administering the caution, including the rank of the officer making the decision, the time between the arrest and the caution

* ensuring the offender understands the nature of the caution, perhaps by a written statement

* encouraging offenders to make contact with medical and drug services where appropriate (7.33)

Other alternatives to prosecution

12.   As with cautioning, we recommend that compounding be extended to drugs other than cannabis. (8.3)

13.   We endorse recommendation 110 of the Royal Commission on Criminal Justice, under which the CPS would be able to require the police to administer a caution in lieu of prosecution, provided that the defendant admitted the offence. (8.7)

14.   We recommend that the CPS and drug agencies adopt a pro-active approach to publicising the criteria for discontinuance on public interest grounds. (8.12)

Health care issues for drug misusers in police custody

15.   Despite the apparent difficulties, we recommend that the treatment options for drug misusers in custody be examined and that jointly-agreed guidelines be developed. (9.6)

16.   From the evidence we have heard, we recognise the difficulties of treating drug misusers in custody. We recommend, however, that good practice requires that:

    1)   If a detainee is already being treated for drug dependence with substitute medication, such as methadone, this should be continued whilst he/she is in custody. Efforts should be made to confirm the current prescription by contacting the doctor and/or clinic concerned, or the retail pharmacist who dispenses the prescription. If the detainee's own medication cannot be obtained, the police surgeon should issue a private prescription.

    2)   If a detainee is not under current treatment (or details of any such treatment cannot be verified) but nevertheless has a clear

history and signs of regular drug use and objective evidence of withdrawal symptoms, treatment should be given to alleviate the severity of withdrawal symptoms.

We recommend that the guidelines in preparation on medical care should incorporate these procedures. (9.7)

17. We recommend piloting the employment of specialist nursing staff in police stations (9.9)

18. We recommend that police surgeons should ask all detainees about the possibility of drug misuse and take the opportunity to put misusers in contact with treatment and rehabilitation agencies. (9.11)

19. We recommend that the Home Office considers ways of clarifying for police surgeons the notification requirements of the relevant Regulations, perhaps in conjunction with the Association of Police Surgeons, and that the guidance being prepared should include reference to this matter. (9.13)

20. We recommend that the professional bodies concerned give consideration to the specific training needs of police surgeons in treating drug misusers. (9.15)

21. We recommend that the HIV/AIDS and Hepatitis B training course being developed for police officers is implemented as a matter of urgency and that progress in this area is monitored by HM Inspectorate of Constabulary. (9.21)

22. We recommend that chief officers explore the possibilities of joint training with local HIV and drugs agencies for their staff. (9.22)

Performance measurement

23. The three main areas of activity in tackling drug misuse which we

recommend the police and other relevant agencies should develop are:

- consultation and the adoption of a common purpose

- development of local, integrated strategies

- application of the principles of harm reduction in the implementation of these strategies (10.5)

24.   In order to monitor police progress in each of these areas we recommend that the HMIC considers posing the following questions as part of the routine inspection process:

- What structure(s) exist within the Force for consultation with other agencies concerning drug misuse?

- Whether a strategy has been devised with other agencies to limit both the demand and supply of drugs?

- And, finally, how enforcement strategies take account of harm reduction and community damage limitation principles? (10.5)

Ethnic Monitoring

25.   We endorse recommendations 2 and 3 of the Royal Commission on Criminal Justice which called for further research into the extent of discrimination against ethnic minorities in the criminal justice system and the introduction of a system of ethnic monitoring to establish how ethnic minorities are treated and identify the measures to ensure that the criminal justice system is applied in the same way to all. (10.7)

26.   We recommend that senior police managers clearly demonstrate the importance which they attach to ethnic monitoring returns and the performance of their forces in this respect, and ensure that the necessary training to achieve this is in place. (10.9)

Appendix A

Background of the Criminal Justice Working Group

The Advisory Council on the Misuse of Drugs (ACMD) was established by the Misuse of Drugs Act 1971 with the duty to keep under review the problems of drug misuse and to advise Ministers on ways of dealing with them. Members of the Council participate in working groups with co-opted experts in relevant fields and report directly to Council at its twice yearly meetings.

The Criminal Justice Working Group was appointed in September 1990 and meets at roughly six weekly intervals. Its initial terms of reference were:

> "To examine and report on aspects of the criminal justice system as they affect drug misusers and on measures to improve their effectiveness. As a first step, to consider and advise in the light of the Government's White Paper on Crime, Justice and Protecting the Public (Cmd 965), on measures to secure effective liaison between the Probation Service and other agencies concerned with the treatment of drug misusing offenders in the community."

The Working Group's Part I Report on 'Community Resources and the Probation Service' was published in November 1991. It has been widely read and has influenced the preparation of national standards in working practices which have been adopted recently by the Probation Service.

In this report the Working Group has considered another important aspect of the criminal justice system.

Appendix B

ADVISORY COUNCIL ON THE MISUSE OF DRUGS:

CRIMINAL JUSTICE WORKING GROUP

Members

Chairman: **Viscountess Runciman OBE** - Citizens' Advice Bureau Community Service, Kensington.

Mr R Bartle JP - Stipendiary Magistrate at Bow Street Magistrates' Court.

Professor P T Bean - Midlands Centre for Criminology and Criminal Justice, Loughborough University.

Mrs J Faugier - Senior Lecturer in School of Nursing Studies, University of Manchester.

Dr P M Fleming - Consultant Psychiatrist and Director, Regional Drug Problem Team, Portsmouth.

Ms J Goodsir - Fellow, Bristol Business School.

Mr P Hayes - Assistant Chief Probation Officer for South East London.

Mr M G Hindson - Assistant Chief Probation Officer for Greater Manchester.

Dr B L Irving - Director, The Police Foundation.

Detective Superintendent H D O'Connell - Head of Drugs Squad, Merseyside Police.

Mr D F O'Connor - Deputy Chief Constable, Kent Constabulary.

Mr K Patel - Bridge Project, Bradford.

Mr M Trace - Project Manager, Parole Release Scheme, London.

Mr D Turner - Director, Standing Conference On Drug Abuse (SCODA).

As chairman of the Council **Professor D G Grahame-Smith** CBE is an ex-officio member of the Group.

Secretary:	Mr J Duke-Evans	Jul '91 - Jan '92
	Mr J Glaze	Jan '92 -
Assistant Secretary:	Miss C Havill	Sep '91 - Aug '92
	Mr C Blairs	Sep '92 - Aug '93
	Mr C Jones	Sep '93 -
Assisted by:	Miss D Williams	

Officials:

Home Office
Mr A Brown
Mrs P Dowdeswell
Mrs K Lidbetter
Mr A D Macfarlane
Miss J Mott
Mr D G Purkiss
Mr P Storr
Mr D Turner
Mr J Woodcock
Mr L P Wright

Department of Health
Dr M Farrell
Ms J Haffenden
Ms C Moriarty
Dr A Thorley

Crown Prosecution Service
Ms M Macdonald
Ms N Reasbeck

SHHD
Mr I Snedden

Appendix C

Evidence submitted to the Working Group

During the preparation of this report, the Working Group took evidence from police working in a range of fields:

Area Drug Squads
Community Affairs
National Criminal Intelligence Service (NCIS)
Senior Management
Street-level enforcement
Training

Other evidence was received from:

Barristers
Crown Prosecution Service
Drug Agencies
Drug Prevention Teams
Local Authorities
Multi-agency Partnerships
Police Surgeons
Residents Associations
The Home Office Drugs Inspectorate
The Voluntary Sector

The Working Group also received presentations of current research in the areas of:

Street-level policing
The care of drug misusers in police custody
Ethnic minority issues
American enforcement methods

We are grateful to the many people and police forces who have provided the Working Group with both written and oral evidence during the course of our enquiries. Without them, our work would have been considerably more difficult.

Printed in the United Kingdom for HMSO
Dd297378 5/94 C25 G3397 10170